During the rehearsals of the first production Rikki Beadle-B~~l~~~~in~~ (right) spoke about *Bashm~~ent~~* with Theatre Royal Press ~~officer~~ Michael Siva and some m~~embers~~ of the original cast.

MICHAEL: What is this play ~~about?~~

RBB: It's about love for music, love for humanity, and the flip side of that, which is hate and self-hatred, fear of music, and fear of humanity.

MICHAEL: What made you write *Bashment*?

RBB: Being involved in this on-going and growing debate about racism among black people, racism in music, racism in Britain, and homophobia in music and Britain, in everyone. It's not just the obvious thing, which is homophobia, but it's also the racism that informs our opinions about these things. It wasn't just a simple thing of, 'Oh, there's a group of people and they don't like gay people'. The debate was so clouded by the way those groups of people were seen by society, the way that society saw itself. It was like the Russian babushka dolls – there was always something else inside the box inside the box inside the box. It was such a complex thing, and I wanted to start opening the boxes inside myself and understanding what I felt about the issue. So, it's a kind of internal debate between these fragments of me. Three years ago, I made a documentary for BBC Radio 4, *Roots of Homophobia*, in which I attempted to trace the homophobia that has recently become rampant in Reggae music back to its source in Jamaica. It turned out to be a painful and complex journey, one that took me through the recording studios and churches of the Caribbean and brought me right back here to the British Isles. Where the laws and religious teachings that informed Jamaican attitudes came from. I debated the issues with my interviewees and even the most vehemently anti-gay told me I'd made them think. The documentary aired. It did well. I got amazing letters, I got awards. People said I'd got them thinking. But nothing really changed – the gay-baiting records multiplied – the 'kill the Battyman' sentiments becoming even more casually confident even as they became more vicious. And then last spring, Brian Williamson, the prominent gay Jamaican activist, was murdered in his own home. And last summer Peter Tatchell's 'Outrage' asked me to join them in an campaign against Ragga music. I admire 'Outrage' – they are the only ones doing something – and something must be done. But still I was conflicted and hesitant about where we would be going or where we were coming from, and was I so ambivalent? Was it because I was black? Was that reining in my gayness? As the press got wind of the issue and the column inches proliferated, I felt my uneasiness increase. I wanted to have a conversation with 'Outrage'. But we were all so busy. Still I wanted to do something. So I wrote this play – to look for the truth to examine the complexity – and to try to do justice to our humanity – all of us – the queerest and the most homophobic (not necessarily mutually exclusive qualities), our humour, our honesty, our hatreds and our hopes. This is not my final word on this subject, but it draws on what I know so far and asks the question that nags at me every day about so many aspects of our lives: What on earth is going on?

MICHAEL: What are your personal views about the use of anti-gay lyrics in dance-hall music?

RBB: They are unnecessary and painful and hurtful, and dangerous, but there are so many things that are painful, hurtful and dangerous in society and yet they exist. Really, my journey has been to try and get past my knee-jerk reaction to those things. I need to get to: how can a record like this be selling so much? Why do people have these feelings? And that takes me to the bigger question. Why do people have these feelings about race, or about women, or about any group in society? Why do people think it's all right to withhold rights, or withhold their own acknowledgement of anybody else's humanity? It makes no sense and yet it can be so widespread. It's not just in Jamaica. It's in America, where they're trying to put anti-gay laws in place right now. Over here, we're just reaching the stage where gay people have equal partnership rights. The idea where somebody can even debate the equality of another human being is shocking to me. I keep thinking about that whole picture, rather than saying, 'Homophobic lyrics – we must stop them'. I want to know where the feelings are coming from and understand that and hopefully, somehow, ease the pain that's causing that.

LUDVIG: As a gay, black man, how did you feel, writing this play?

RBB: I found it hard to understand why people beat each other up. I found it hard to confront, but it was good for me. I found the anger and the hatred really hard. Trying to get all my feelings about it, and the debates that I have, all into a play, that was hard. It wasn't difficult to do, but rather painful to do. It was a challenge, but a painful challenge. But the things that make me want to write are the things that I don't understand. Somebody said to me the other day, 'Everything you do has loads of drugs in it'. I thought to myself, No, it doesn't! This play doesn't, for instance. But I thought back to the last five or six things I'd written and there's loads of drugs in them. And I've never taken a single drug. But to me, it's my way of trying to understand it, do get it, appreciate it and not just put myself above it. Violence in there is not part of my life, but I want to understand it. I want to bring myself closer to people that I don't relate to.

Theatre Royal
STRATFORD EAST
'a pioneering theatre' New York Times

presents

Bashment

by Rikki Beadle-Blair

Performing at Theatre Royal Stratford East
20 May – 18 June 2005
restaged 29 September – 22 October 2005

Theatre Royal Stratford East
Gerry Raffles Square
Stratford
London
E15 1BN

www.stratfordeast.com

Theatre Royal
└─STRATFORD EAST─┘
'a pioneering theatre' New York Times

Cast in order of speaking

JJ **Joel Dommett**
Orlando **Anthony Newell**
MC Eggy **Jason Steed**
White Fang **Davie Fairbanks**
(originally played by Joe Marshall)
MC Venom **Ludvig Bonin**
MC KKK **Nathan Clough**
Karisma **Jennifer Daley**
Sam **Arnie Hewitt**
Daniel **Elliott James-Fisher**
(originally played by Luke Toulson)
Kevan **Duncan MacInnes**
Bashment Compere **Arnie Hewitt**
Arresting Officer, Judge, Prison Officer **Elliott James-Fisher**

Musician **Joni Levinson**

Creative Team

Written & Directed by **Rikki Beadle-Blair**
Set & Lighting Design **Giuseppe di Iorio**
Sound Design **Gareth Owen**
Music composed by **Rikki Beadle-Blair**
'How do you love me' performed by **Rikki**, **Joni Levinson** &
Antoine Stone
Bashment music performed by **Antoine Stone** & **Rikki**
Engineered and co-produced by **Antoine Stone**
Costume Design **Fola Solanke**
Graffiti Art by **John Gordon**
Assistant Manager on the book **Altan Reyman**

Performing at Theatre Royal Stratford East
20 May – 18 June 2005
restaged 29 September – 22 October 2005

JASON: Which character in *Bashment* did you most enjoy writing about?

RBB: There wasn't one in particular. There isn't a favourite character to write about, because they're all fragments of me. They're all parts of me.

JASON: Is that how you write generally, in all your plays?

RBB: Yeah, not consciously, but I've become very aware, very quickly, that they're all bits of me, arguing with each other. No matter how unpleasant what they say is, you can't write something more unpleasant than what you would think of. There's always something that's hiding in you that you're questioning, or challenging, or revealing.

JOEL: What do you want your audience to get out of it?

RBB: I want them to think. I would like people to judge each other less, though you can't erase judgments. People do bad things, but I would like people to judge each other less and relate to each other more, because I think that's the answer to the conflict, to understand each other more.

ARNIE: Do you think that people coming to see *Bashment* will be coming more to see a musical than a serious play?

RBB: I worried a lot about the title, but it's so strong, because it covers the music and it has 'bashing' in it, so it seems absolutely the right title. The celebration of music in the play is about my love for music, as well as my disappointment in the message that music can bring, or the way that people can use it. All the way through the play, the love of the music is expressed in the characters, though it's not a musical. I love writing musicals, but that's not what this is. It's a play about music, rather than a play done through music.

JOEL: Are you aiming to write a play that's naturalistic?

RBB: I admire naturalistic film-makers hugely. Ken Loach is a genius. But it's not me. That's not what I do. Dreams, to me, are the reality, and people tell the truth through their dreams. That's when you can't control what you're feeling. To me, theatre and art and film are like hyper-real things. Take Chagall's *The Birthday*. You have a girl, it's her birthday, she's holding a cake, he's kissing her, but he's upside down floating in the air and she's kind of off the ground, coming away from the cooker. To me, that's what captures what it's like to be in love with somebody and they've made you a birthday cake and you kissed them. You feel as if you're ten feet off the ground. It's not real, but it's honest. I'm not interested in naturalism. The thing of having them debating, I had to surrender to that to a degree and say, it's okay to do political theatre that involves discussion, because this subject needs discussion. The thing that's going wrong between the characters in the play is that they haven't experienced discussion up to now about it. I wanted to start the discussion. The characters would discuss the issue in the play; hopefully the audience would discuss it in the foyer, the critics would discuss it in the papers and people would start thinking about it.

JASON: Who inspired you to write originally, back in the day?

RBB: My mum. She taught me to read and write, before I went to school. So, when I was three, I started to read and I immediately wanted to be a writer. I think it was all those books in the library. There was a kind of magic world in the library and I wanted to just be a part of that world. All these people had so much to say, so many words and it was so exciting, I've still never written anything that's been in a library, but to me that's incredibly exciting. I just wanted to do that. Now, what inspires me to write is a good writer, especially American ones, but the thing that really inspires me are paintings and good song-writers. But what inspires me the most to write are actors, which is why I tend to cast things before I write them. I can go into situations where I don't know what I'm going to say, what I'm going to write, but I know that if somebody's passionate about their craft and if someone's a good actor, it makes me desperate to hear them say my lines, so I find something for them to say.

MICHAEL: Which part of Jamaica is your mother from?

RBB: My mother's a big-town gal from Kingston! She was actually there at the same time when I did my documentary on her own little trip. So, I met up with her a couple of times. She was very, very, very excited that I was there finally, in Jamaica, and she wanted me to enjoy the beauty of the place and the people. She was concerned about the homophobia in the music, but she didn't want me to just see Jamaica in that light. She really wanted me to celebrate it, so it was quite difficult for her, I think. It was as complicated for her, with me being there and doing this documentary, as it was for me.

MICHAEL: Could you tell us a bit about your previous work?

RBB: I did a TV series called *Metrosexuality*. It was about a community in West London, which was black, white, gay, straight – every sexuality and colour in between. That's still playing all around the world. I've worked on a radio series of my own where I've played characters. Every day I'd play a different character, and I'd have a guest actor with me playing a guest character. Radio was great, because I could play anything and do anything, and what I looked like didn't get in the way. I played a dog once; my dog Angelica, and then I played a racist taxi driver who turned out to be black. I did a movie called *Stonewall* for BBC and an American company. That was great, because that brought me to the attention to the Americans, and I was very lucky to have that. I'm the executive story editor for a TV series in America right now called *Noah's Ark*. I just wrote a musical down at the Oval House called *Prettyboy*, and my company, 'Angelica', is resident over at the Actors Centre, and hopefully resident in other places as well. I'm looking for work, so we can word this like a personal ad, you know – 'Actor/writer/director/composer likes long walks and making art. Looking for theatres and film companies for a lasting relationship.' I just love to work, and I do a lot of work. I've got a big output in a lot of different areas. I can't be busy enough. Time is short. You've got to create.

MICHAEL: What plans do you have for the future after *Bashment*?

RBB: I'm doing a stage version of *Stonewall*, which I'm adapting now for the Pleasance Theatre. I'm doing another two productions for the Axis Centre. One's called *Human*, which is a romantic comedy between people who have terminal illnesses. Hopefully, I'm going to do more plays here in London, and then I'm off to America. Of course, the thing I do every year is I work with young filmmakers in South Africa, helping them make their first films. I've done this for two years, making short films. Next year, I'm hoping to get three directors together to make a feature.

MICHAEL: How do you feel this play reflects Stratford East's commitment to develop new talent and new voices?

RBB: This play is a poster for Stratford East's policies, which I applaud, because I was able to use a completely new cast. For most of these actors, it is their first professional theatre job. So, they're all unknown actors, who I've written the play for, and they've very kindly let me do that. And actually, this is only my second writing job for theatre. I've written lots and lots of television and radio, and film, and been paid lots of money for that! But this is only my second paid professional writing job in London for theatre. So, I'm new talent! We have a first-time costume designer, we have a racially diverse cast, and I think we're going to have a lot of first-time audience members as well. The subject matter of the play is something we deliberately chose to bring young people into the theatre, so they can see that it can be as relevant as cinema like *Bullet Boy* or the TV programmes that they watch and the music they listen to.

The way I work, by Rikki Beadle-Blair

Of course the exact details of the process depend on the project – when other companies ask me to write for them, especially when I am not the director, I usually work in the way that suits the organisation or person who I'm working for. Invariably this means we talk, I write, they give notes and I rewrite and rewrite until they feel the script is ready to shoot, or be staged, or sent to Development Hell.

I have no problems working this way – in fact, it can be fun – but when I am the writer/director, as with this play, I prefer to cast the piece first and then write specifically for the cast. They are usually a combination of people who I have worked with for a long time, newish people who have done one or two productions or participated in readings and workshops along with brand new actors who have written to me recently and invited me along to see their work. If they capture my imagination and manage to keep themselves on my radar, I eventually call them up and ask if I can write a part for them. Once I have enough yeses, (you'd be surprised how many people are too busy to have a play written for them), we get together and sit round a table. I tell them what the play is likely to be about (if I know) and then we chat, possibly about the subject matter, but more probably about a wandering range of random subjects... At the end of the first session the actors choose their characters' names and sometimes answer ten random questions about their characters – and then I go away and start to write.

We meet for the chats perhaps once a week for a month of two, and, hopefully, to read the latest instalment. It unfolds like a weekly soap, all of us curious to see what on earth will happen next. Suddenly, eventually I feel ready to bind the pages and we have a script, we have a play! Or at least a first draft. And we start to rehearse. And talk. And I rewrite and rewrite and rewrite, the poor cast highlighting their lines in script after script only to throw them away that same day.

So far, this process has not involved any improvising – though I'm not ruling it out for the future – but their presence and group dynamic is crucial to the development of the play. As I sample their 'personality DNA' I find that my usual themes and obsessions are informed with unexpected triggers that are sparked by the personalities, strengths, limitations and physical attributes of the actors I am working with. They are not playing themselves, by any means; they are often required to transform themselves quite dramatically and sometimes traumatically. They fill in extensive questionnaires in character, we do field trips to research accents and character histories as we try to create as total a synthesis between the actor and the character and keep on interrogating the script and myself and rewriting... The cast is a crucial element. They don't write the play – but it would be a totally different creation without them... Let me take this moment to thank every actor who has allowed me to write a part for them – You are my muses. My source of inspiration and revelation. And I cannot wait to see what you make happen next.

If you want to work with Rikki or ask a question – please email:
RikkiBB@aol.com

BASHMENT – our Youth Theatre's perspective

What do you know about Bashment?

Jamal (16yrs): *I've been listening to it for about seven years, It's been around for about ten to twelve years.*

What attracts you to it?

Jamal: *I like the beat, the lyrics and the names of the dances they make up. Some of the lyrics are offensive, cussing people – homophobic. I feel kind of sorry for them, but they cover it up with good songs and a good beat. It's mostly young people that listen to it. The best clubs are in the West End and Essex.*

I hear you like Bashment

Monique (17yrs): *24// me. Back, back...it came from reggae, (She sings.) but now it's harder, (She sings.) the lyrics are changed. Nowadays it's more about the music. You hear it more now on mainstream radio. I'm probably attracted to it 'cause my family are Jamaican...that's where it comes from. The lyrics can be quite explicit. I listen to the rhythm, not really the words. It can be against gays. Could be offensive. They come across like that, raw, they're not intending to be that hard, it's because they've been brought up like that, their religion...it's just their belief. It's about dancing, having a laugh, a lively beat. Nowadays the men do most of the dancing...shake an arm...put their all into it. I don't go to clubs as much...the garage music...it can get out of hand.*

What attracts you to Bashment?

Angelique (18yrs): *I like the beat. Now they've created new dance movements like 'Signal the Plane'. My favourite is "pon the river, 'pon the bank...' It's a leg movement one.*

Who does it appeal to?

Angelique: *Teenagers up to 35 years, quite a wide range actually.*

Who are the artists you like?

Angelique: *The best ones are Elephant Man, Vibez Kartel, Sizzla... Most come from Jamaica and come over here... I don't know any British-born ones. I know some people don't like the lyrics. Some people have certain beliefs. Like they don't believe in gay...and if you are gay it could be offensive. I listen to the music and move to the beat...that's what I enjoy. If I took a gay friend to a club, I'd tell them first...that some of them have issues. Some lyrics talk about killing them off. As I said, I like the beat.*

What does Bashment mean to you?

Charlene (18yrs): *Bashment attracts all ages really. I like the beat, the energy...it's happy music really. You can do what you want. Some have been invented like Scooby Doo, it's the artists on stage that get you dancing really. I can't understand all the lyrics, because of the speed and the lingo. There's some anti-gay ones. It's quite light-hearted. It's good fun and good energy.*

Interviewed Thursday 21 April 2005

CAST in order of speaking

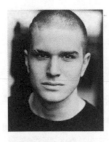

Joel Dommett JJ

Bashment is 19-year-old Joel's second play with Rikki Beadle-Blair, the first being *Gutted* at the Tristan Bates Theatre playing Luke Prospect. This was part of the *Passion Plays* trilogy shown last year. Joel also played Michael in *Unity 1918* at the Old Vic and Bobby in *The Visit* at Bristol Old Vic. TV credits include: *Casualty* (BBC), *Watch Over Me 2* (BBC), *Totally Frank* (Channel 4) and *Golden Hour* (ITV). In 2004 Joel also played Conan in *Jam*, a film by Angelo Abaela due to be released this year.

Anthony Newell Orlando

Anthony has a BA (Hons) in Drama from London Metropolitan University. He began performing with The Theatre Royal Plymouth's Young Company, performing in London, Devon and Poland. Professional credits include: *Yerma's Eggs* (Riverside Studios); *Sweet* (Tristan Bates Theatre); *The Mousetrap* (European no.1 tour); *Persius* (UK tour); *Crazyblack-motherfuckingself* readings (Soho Theatre & the Royal Court); *Prettyboy* (Oval House Theatre); *Jack and the Beanstalk* (Elgiva Theatre); and *The Peach Child* (The Little Angel Theatre). Film credit: *Jimmy's Story,* a short film for the Media Trust. Anthony has presented for Longbow Productions, and later this year will be filming his first feature film: *Rogue Stars*.

Jason Steed MC Eggy

Training credits at ALRA include: *Machinal Widows* and *Richard III*. Jason's professional theatre credits include: *Laters* (Tristan Bates Theatre) and a no.1 Tour of the hard-hitting Jamaican comedy *Passa Passa*. His television work includes: *Silent Witness* (BBC); *The Courtroom* (Mersey TV). Film work includes: *Urban Peacocks* and the lead Danny in the shortfilm *Punchbag*, which has been recently selected for the BFI-Blackworld Festival.

Davie Fairbanks White Fang

Taken under the wing of Rikki Beadle-Blair at the tender age of 17, Davie has worked on a number of acting and musical projects. Finding his feet for acting in Fringe Theatre, he landed his first screen role in the pilot episode of *Hetrosexuality* as the character Bambi, and soon after in the follow on hit series *Metrosexuality* for Channel 4. In 2002 Davie worked with Rikki on a feature of *Superhero* (Post Production) in which he played the character Connor. Continuing with his own writing inspired by Rikki, Davie was lucky enough to work as an additional writer on *Kidulthood*, a feature due out later this year.

Ludvig Bonin MC Venom

Ludvig attended The Academy of Live and Recorded Arts (ALRA) where he trained for three years to become a professional actor. Training credits include: Michael in *The Good Hope*; Alexis in *Widows* and Chris in *The Beau Defeated*, all performed in the Leon Eagle Theatre. Theatre credits include: *Sweet Love Adieu* (Bowen West Theatre / Bedford Park) and *Laters* (Tristan Bates Theatre). Television credits include: TV licensing commercial and *EastEnders* (both for the BBC).

Nathan Clough MC KKK

Nathan trained at the Academy of Live and Recorded Arts. Training credits include: *The Mill on The Floss*, *Angels in America*; *The Ghost Train* (Leon Eagles Theatre). Professional credits include: Romeo in *Romeo and Juliet* (Wycombe Swan); Sykes Jones in *Sweat* (The Space); Macbeth in *Macbeth* (The Broadway Studio, Catford); Duane in *Laters* (Tristan Bates Theatre); Gratiano in *The Merchant of Venice* (Wycombe Swan, The Broadway Studio); Talthybius/Menelaus in *The Women of Troy* (Wycombe Swan, The Broadway Studio); *Wide Asleep* (Arcola Theatre) and the stage tour of *Gun Play* (Big Fish Theatre Company). Film credits include: *Trust*, *A View from the Bar* and the award winning feature film *Lovestruck*.

Jennifer Daley Karisma

Jennifer Trained at the Webber Douglas Academy of Dramatic Art and has a BA (Hons) in Performing Arts from Middlesex University. Since leaving drama school, television credits include: Carolyn Bailey in *Doctors* (BBC), Joanne in *Casualty* (BBC), Alison in *Packhorse* (Sony Media). Theatre credits include: Sunai in *Gutted – The South London Passion Plays*, also by Rikki Beadle-Blair; *The London Exiles* 2 revue at the Soho Theatre, *Electra* at the Young Vic Studio and Sunna in *Unity 1918*, as part of a rehearsed reading of Canadian plays at the Old Vic.

Arnie Hewitt Sam

Arnie trained at the Birmingham School of Speech and Drama and grew up in Nottingham.

He has worked extensively with Young People's Theatre Companies such as Merseyside Young People's Theatre Co, Halfmoon Theatre Company and Theatre Centre where he recently had the pleasure of working with the acclaimed Jamaican British Poet Benjamin Zephaniah. In 2003 Arnie added a new string to his bow working for The Little Angel Puppet Theatre Company, touring with their very successful show *Go Noah Go* based on Noah's Ark in which he and one other actor provided all the voices for over fifty animals in the show. Arnie is also a dancer, and has worked for The Spice Girls and Radio One road shows such as *Party in the Park*, dancing for over 20,000 people. Television includes a three-part special for *The Bill*. Arnies's theatre credits for 2004 include playing the role of Mowgli in the highly successful Theatre Royal Northampton production of *Jungle Book* and Katya in *Pinocchio* for Artsdepot. This is Arnie's first time at Theatre Royal Stratford East and he is thrilled to be working here.

Elliott James-Fisher Daniel

Elliott graduated from Arts Educational School of Acting four years ago. His first professional stage role was in Sir Peter Hall's production of *Bacchai* at the National Theatre. He has continued to perform on the London stage at the Soho Theatre, Blue Elephant Theatre, The Courtyard Theatre, The Landor and the Tristan Bates Theatre where he worked closely with Rikki Beadle-Blair on several productions before being cast in *Bashment*. Earlier this year Elliott worked with Rik Mayall in *Violent Nation* – a documentary about violence in the UK and has just returned from a successful run of a show *!Runners... The Return* at the Edinburgh Fringe Festival, which received critical acclaim and was nominated for the best new writing by the Writer's Guild.

Duncan MacInnes Kevan

Duncan trained at The Liverpool Institute for Performing Arts (LIPA). Recent theatre credits include: Rudd in *Murder With Love* and Rupert Brook in *Deadly Lovers* both for Theatre Royal (Nottingham), Kevan in the original cast production of *Bashment* for the Theatre Royal Stratford East, Mickey P in *The South London Passion Plays* and Christian in *Move* (Tristan Bates Theatre); Kent in *Edward II* (The Royal National Theatre Studios); Tabaqui in *The Jungle Book* (The Chester Gateway); *Pacific Overtures* for which he won a Scotsman Award for the role of Tamate (Assembly Rooms, Edinburgh); Mamilius in *The Winter's Tale* (The English Shakespeare Company). Film credits include: Aaron in *Little Boy's Lies* (Grindstone Films). Duncan is currently writer in residence at the Theatre Train Stage School with projects including *Eastside* and *Travelling Without Leaving*, soon to be performed at the Shaw Theatre later this summer.

CREATIVES

Rikki Beadle-Blair Writer & Director

Rikki Beadle-Blair was born and raised in South London, where he attended Lois Acton's Experimental Bermondsey Lampost Free School. He wrote his first play aged seven and began directing aged eleven. After a diverse career, that often spilled out of the world of fringe theatre to take in six months in a Baghdad Cabaret, performing in a snake act across the UK, choreographing Brazilian strippers, Rikki co-founded the Rock Band 'Boysie', garnering a large following on the London gig circuit. Meanwhile, due to his cult success work in the theatre Rikki was hired to write movie *Stonewall* for BBC and the US indie film company, Killer Films. The movie, directed by Nigel Finch, went on to win the audience awards at the London Film Festival and the San Francisco Lesbian and Gay film festival as well an award for Rikki at Outfest LA for Outstanding Screenwriting. Among other television projects, Rikki wrote, directed and featured in the hugely successful Channel 4 series *Metrosexuality* as well as composing the soundtrack. He has also worked extensively for BBC Radio 4, writing and performing his own series of plays. His documentary *Roots of Homophobia* won the Sony award for Best Radio Feature. His Theatre Company 'Angelica' is resident at the Tristan Bates Theatre in Covent Garden which has hosted previews of his *South London Passion Plays* trilogy. *Gutted*, *Laters* and *Sweet* detailing the lives and loves of Rudeboys and Chavs in Bermondsey. Other plays developed there in this fruitful period have been *Move* set at the time of Soho bombings and *Human* in which a love affair between two people with only nine months to live, acted by a different couple every night portraying characters of widely varying races, sexes, sexualities and social backgrounds. These plays from the Tristan Bates are among his proudest achievements and Rikki intends to develop them all further. Rikki's other recent work includes composing and directing the musical *Prettyboy* at Oval House Theatre, where he also directed Matt Harris's *Venom,* writing *Gunplay* for Big Fish Theatre Company and writing and directing *Ask & Tell* for the National Youth Theatre. He is currently adapting *Stonewall* as a stage production for The Pleasance Theatre and working on a new play *Eden,* set in a Soho Hostess Bar. He works part of the year in Los Angeles as the Executive Story Editor for *Noah's Arc*, the first Gay Black TV Series, and works part of the year in South Africa creating debut films with first-time filmmakers as a director for the 'Out in Africa' organisation. Rikki's next play *Totally Practically Naked in My Bedroom on a Wednesday Night* opens three days after this production and closes on Oct 25 at the Tristan Bates Theatre. Contact: RikkiBB@aol.com

Giuseppe di Iorio Set & Lighting Designer

Giuseppe was born in Naples and trained at Guildhall School of Music and Drama, London. His recent lighting designs include: *Romeo and Juliet* for British Youth Opera (Peacock Theatre, London); *The Women of Troy* (Cryptic Theatre, Glasgow); *Little Red Riding Hood* by George Apergis for Almeida Opera Festival (2005); *Macbeth* and *La Sonnambula* for Holland Park Opera (2005); *Bastiano e Bastiana/La Serva Padrona* (Lugo Opera Festival); *La Bohème* for Opera Zuid (Holland); *A Handful of Dust* (Citizen Theatre Glasgow); *The Knot Garden* (Scottish Opera); *Gli Amici di Salamanca* (Teatro Comunale, Bologna); three opera productions for Wexford Opera Festival (2004, 2002 and 2001): *Elsa Canasta* by J De Frutos (Rambert Dance Company), *The Barber of Seville* and *Marriage of Figaro* (Savoy Opera); *Rabbit*, a new play for Frantic Assembly (Lyric Hammersmith and national tour); *Aida* (Scottish Opera); *Simon Boccanegra* (Teatro Verdi, Trieste); *Aida* (Teatro Lirico di Cagliari); *Faust* and the world premiere of

Romanza (Opera di Roma); *King Priam* and *Turn of the Screw* for Nationale ReisOper (Holland); *Xerxes* and the world premiere of *The Possessed* by Haris Vrondos (Greek National Opera); *La Traviata* (Malmo Opera). His recent set and lighting designs include: *Semele* (Scottish Opera); *Otello* (Oper Kiel); *Macbeth* (Oper Muenster); *Il Trovatore* (Oper Nurnberg); *An Evening with Apergis* (Royal Festival Hall London); *The Emperor of Atlantis* by Viktor Ullmann, co-designed with John Fulljames (site specific promenade at Kilmainham Gaol, Dublin for Opera Theatre Company), winner of Best Opera Production at the Irish Theatre Award 2002; *Orphee*, *Marathon* and *Vasco* (Klesidra, Rome / London / Edinburgh). Future projects include lighting designs: Die *Zauberflute* for Bolshoi Theatre of Russia (Moscow); *Charlotte's Web* for Citizen Theatre (Glasgow); *Manon* and *Turn of the Screw* (Nationale ReisOper, Holland).

Gareth Owen for Orbital Sound Design

Gareth has an honours degree in Underwater Science from Plymouth University and is a full-time Sound Designer for London's Orbital Sound. Gareth's current and most recent theatre shows include: *Thoroughly Modern Millie* (UK Tour), *The Olivier Awards* (Park Lane Hilton), *Jesus Christ Superstar* (Danish National Tour), Lily Savage's *Snow White and The Seven Dwarfs* (West End), *Fame* (UK National Tour), *Beauty and The Beast* (Sound Effects Design, UK National Tour), and *Love Shack* (Associate Designer, UK National Tour). Past theatre highlights include: *Tick Tick Boom* (Broadway), RSC Winter Season (West End), *Evita* (Beirut), *The Rocky Horror Show* (UK National Tour & West End), *Noise Ensemble* (Edinburgh Festival), *GodSpell* (UK National Tour), Barbara Cooke's *Broadway* (West End), *Guys & Dolls* (European Tour), *West Side Story* (MTG), *Calamity Jane* (UK National Tour), *Miss Saigon* (UK National Tour), *Summer Holiday* (UK National Tour), *Secret Rapture* (West End), *Bombshell* (West End), *Fully Committed* (West End), *Jesus Christ Superstar* (Porchester Castle), *Blues Brothers* (West End), *Grease* (Cyprus), *Romeo & Juliet* (West End), *Slamdunk* (National Tour & German Tour), *Double Cross* (West End), *Stones in their Pockets* (UK National Tour), *Merce Cunningham* (Tate Modern), *Murderer* (Chocolate Factory), *The Olivier Awards 04* (Park Lane Hilton), *Red Priest* (Hackney), *Camelot* (Regents Park), *The Big Life* (Stratford), *The Battle of Green Lanes* (Stratford) and over twenty QDos and Paul Elliott Pantomimes. Gareth began his career in the rock & roll world and has been lucky enough to work with artistes from Anastasia all the way through to The Zutons. Highlights along the way have included Elton John, The Stereophonics, Paul Young, and BB King. Gareth's written work is regularly published worldwide in both *AudioMedia* and *Pro Sound News Magazine*. Every year he teaches the National Sound Design Course for the National Theatre, as well as several courses for the ABTT (Association of British Theatre Technicians).

Fola Solanke Costume Designer

Fola graduated and has a Higher Diploma Fashion Design at London college of Fashion. Her credits include: BP Statemanship/Hawkshead (2005, Corporate Video); as wardrobe supervisor for *Foyles War* 1V'; *The Bullet Boy*. As costume assistant for *Wondrous Oblivion* (2002, Wondrous Oblivion Ltd); *Merlin* (1998 Mysterious Passions Ltd); *Little Bird* (2000, Granada Television); *The Grimleys*; *Storm Damage* (1998, BBC Drama); *Mother Teresa – In the Name of God's Poor* (1997, Hallmark); *Peggy Su* (Decco Films). As standby costume for *High Heels, Lowlife* (2000 Fragile Films/Buena Vista). As costume designer for *Out* (2000, A-Z Films).

Joni Levinson Musician

Joni trained in drama at the City Literary Institute. He is a member of Kindle Improv Theatre Group, and his theatre credits include: Telegin in *Uncle Vanya*, and most recently, 'A' in *Human* (Tristan Bates). He played Gabriel in Channel 4's *Metrosexuality*, and Eric in *Superhero* – a digital feature to be released later this year. He provided musical accompaniment for Rikki Beadle-Blair's *Passion Plays*, and played guitar and keyboard in Rikki's *Prettyboy*. He is open to all offers.

THEATRE ROYAL STRATFORD EAST AND
SHEFFIELD THEATRES PRESENT

GLADIATO

PREVIEWS 2 NOV · 1.30PM · 3 NOV · 1.30PM
£5 BEST AVAILABLE SEATS

DEATH iN FELTHAM.
WHY WAS ZAHiD MUBAREK KiLLED?

**POST-SHOW DISCUSSIONS WILL FOLLOW EVERY EVENING
PERFORMANCE.** Theatre Royal is bringing together a
panel of guests and experts to discuss issues raised by
the Zahid Mubarek case and related to Gladiator Games.
Please check our website for who is on the panel each night.

R GAMES

Dramatised by **Tanika Gupta**

On the eve of his release from Feltham Young Offenders Institution *Zahid Mubarek*, a young British Asian man, was attacked by his cellmate. One week later he died of his injuries. How was this allowed to happen?

This new play traces his family's pursuit of the truth. Based on interviews and accounts given to the Feltham Inquiry, one of Britain's leading writers examines the incompetence of the official response to *Zahid Mubarek's* death.

Director Charlotte Westenra
Designer Paul Wills
Lighting Designer Hartley T A Kemp

Cast to be announced

2nd - 12th November 2005

Time: Tues - Sat 7.30pm
Mattinees: 3, 8 & 9 at 1.30pm
and 12 at 3pm

Signed performance:
Thurs 10th Nov, 7.30pm.
Audio described performance:
Fri 11th Nov, 7.30pm.

Tickets: £8, £12, £16 & £20
Concessions HALF PRICE!

Special discount for schools and colleges:
Book 10 or more tickets for any Tues, Wed or Thurs show for just £4 a seat!

Discussion following every evening performance

Pinocchio

By **Trish Cooke** and **Robert Hyman**

'Enough wit and charm
to cut through the worst
Christmas hangover'

EVENING STANDARD

'Stratford East has always led the field in Christmas shows'

WHAT'S ON IN LONDON

The cautionary tale of a small boy with a big nose is this year's pantomime at Theatre Royal Stratford East.

Yes, Pinocchio, that naughty puppet with a conscience (*and boy does he need one!*) comes to our famous old stage with a show full of excitement, laughter, sing-along songs and that unique magic that can only be found in a Stratford East panto.

What makes it so magical? Why you the audience of course, the liveliest in town. So make sure you are there to play your part and book your tickets now!

Director Kerry Michael
Assistant Director Jamie Beddard
Designer Jenny Tiramani
Choreographer Jason Pennycooke
Lighting Designer Paul Anderson

Cast to be announced

Mon-Sat - 26th Nov 2005 - 21st Jan 2006

For full list of dates and time of shows please visit our web site www.stratfordeast.com or ring 020 8534 0310.

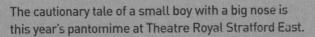 **Signed performance:**
Thurs 15th Dec, 1.30pm
Thurs 5th Jan, 1.30pm
Sat 7th Jan, 3 & 7.15pm

Audio described performance:
Sat 10th Dec, 3 & 7.15pm

[TXT] **Captioned performance:**
Thur 19th Jan,
1.30 & 7.15pm

Tickets: £8, £12, £16 & £20
Concessions HALF PRICE!

Theatre Royal
—STRATFORD EAST—
'a pioneering theatre' New York Times

Production Credits

Fight Director	Bret Yount
Make-up Consultant	Amy Skinner
Followspot	Phil Emerson, Gemma Neve
Fly Men	Ron Hardman, Dave Munday, Ben Ranner

Theatre Royal
STRATFORD EAST

'a pioneering theatre' New York Times

Theatre Royal Stratford East Staff

Artistic
Artistic Director — Kerry Michael
Associate Director — Dawn Reid
New Writing Associate — Ashmeed Sohoye
New Writing Project Manager — Sita Ramamurthy
Assistant to Artistic Director — Katja Janus
Writer In Residence — Hope Massiah
Senior Script Associate — Myra Brenner
Theatre Archivist — Murray Melvin
Assistant Archivist — Mary Ling

Associate Artists — ULTZ, Clint Dyer
Musical Theatre Associate Artists — Fred Carl, Suzanne Gorman, Robert Lee, Paulette Randall, Deborah Sathe, Zoe Simpson

Administration
Executive Director — Tim Highman
Associate Producer — Karen Fisher
Development Director — Elizabeth Royston
Development Officer — Kathryn Williams
Development Consultant — Dilshani Weerasinghe
Finance Manager — Paul Canova
Finance Officer — Elinor Jones

Youth Arts
Head of Youth Arts — Jan Sharkey-Dodds
Youth Arts Officer — Karlos Coleman
Projects Administrator — Phil Emerson

Marketing and Press
Head of Marketing and Sales — Barry Burke
Marketing Officer — Silvia Pilotto
Press Officer — Michael Siva
Audience Development Manager — Kilian Gideon
Box Office Manager — Beryl Warner
Box Office Assistants — Asha Bhatti, Davina Campbell, Alice Cooke, Sharleen Fulgence, Sarah Wheeler

Photography — Johnny Munday

Production

Production Manager	Chris Robinson
Head of Stage	Ben Ranner
Stage Manager	Helen Gaynor
Deputy Stage Manager	Gwyn D Jenkins
Assistant Stage Manager	Altan Reyman
Assistant Stage Manager	Rebecca Clatworthy
Chief Electrician	Stuart Saunders
Deputy Chief Electrician	Dave Karley
Wardrobe Supervisor	Isolde Walker

Front of House

Theatre Manager	Terry O'Dwyer
Duty Manager	Sharleen Fulgence, Lynsey Webb, Liz Okinda
Maintenance	Daniel Harty
Bar Manager	Graeme Bright
Bar Assistants	Doyin Akinola, Christopher Anipole, Dawn Dunn, John Karley, Piotr Klaczek, Kemisha Plummer, Ysanne Tidd
Domestic Assistants	Julie Lee, Helen Mepham, Magdalena Sobczynska, Jane Young, Lynsey Webb
Fire Marshals	Kofi Agyemang-Prempeh, Daniel Harty, Liz Okinda, Rameeka Parvez, Lynsey Webb
Ushers	Kofi Agyemang-Prempeh, Emma Ballard, Cynthia Erivo, Doreen Friend, Sonia Gittens, James Gray, Rebecca Howell, Avita Jay, Ashley Marquis, Noshid Miah, Liz Okinda, Lola Olokodana, Sade Olokodana, Rameeka Parvez, Jessie Rawlinson, Jalil Saheeb, Magdalena Sobcynska, Katy Winterflood

Refugees and The Arts Initiative	Nela Milic (The Refugees and the Arts Initiative is an independent organization that is hosted by Theatre Royal Stratford East)
Board of Directors	Sally Banks, Clint Dyer, Bonnie Greer, Tony Hall (*Chair*), John Lock, Jo Martin, Murray Melvin (*Company Secretary*), John Newbigin, Paul O'Leary, Shannen Owen, Mark Pritchard, Sarah Smith (*Treasurer*), Matthew Xia

Theatre Royal
STRATFORD EAST
'a pioneering theatre' New York Times

Contacting the Theatre

Theatre Royal Stratford East
Gerry Raffles Square
Stratford
London
E15 1BN

e-mail theatreroyal@stratfordeast.com
Website www.stratfordeast.com

Free Booking Line 0800 183 1188
Information line 020 8534 0310
Administration 020 8534 7374
Fax 020 8534 8381
Minicom 020 8279 1114
Press Direct Line 020 8279 1123
Education Direct Line 020 8279 1107

Offices open	Mon – Fri	10am – 6pm
Box Office open	Mon – Sat	10am – 7pm
Bar open	Mon – Sat	11am – 11pm
	Sunday	12am – 10.30pm
Food served	Monday	12.30pm – 9.30pm
	Tues – Sun	12.30pm – 7.30pm

Caribbean Flavours in the Theatre Royal Bar

The finest fish and chicken spiced and cooked to perfection by our chef, Wills, as well as a wide range of non-Caribbean food, salads and snacks. Now available in the Theatre Royal Bar.

Thanks to the supporters of the Theatre Royal

We thank the major supporters of Theatre Royal Stratford East for their continuing support: Arts Council England, London Borough of Newham, the Association of London Government and Channel 4 to support our work to develop new musicals.

We would also like to thanks the Funders and Supporters of Theatre Royal Stratford East: Big Lottery Community Fund, Bridge House Estates Trust Fund, Calouste Gulbenkian Foundation, Cultural Industries Development Agency, Clothworkers Build, Equity Trust Fund, European Social Fund, Financial Services Authority, The Foundation for Sport and the Arts, Help a London Child, Jack Petchey Foundation, Ken Hill Trust, Mackintosh Foundation, Mercers' Company, PRS Foundation, Pidem Fund, UBS Investment Bank and Unity Theatre Trust.

BASHMENT

for John Gordon

First published in 2005 by Oberon Books Ltd
521 Caledonian Road, London N7 9RH
Tel: 020 7607 3637 / Fax: 020 7607 3629
e-mail: oberon.books@btconnect.com
www.oberonbooks.com

New edition, 2005

A catalogue record for this book is available from the British Library.

ISBN: 1 84002 582 4

Cover design by Nick Mosley
Photography by Rikki Beadle-Blair

Printed in Great Britain by Antony Rowe Ltd, Chippenham

Characters

JJ
21 year old Bristol-born white boy – low-key hip-hop styling – quiet, determined

ORLANDO
21 year old Bristol-born and white – arty, bohemian, feminine, intelligent

MC EGGY
23 year old East London-born African, muscular, Ragga MC – protective

WHITE FANG
20 year old Jewish middleclass mockney who chats blackney – cocky

MC VENOM
21 year old East London-born African – compact fit Ragga DJ – nervy

MC KKK
22 year old East London-born Jamaican – wiry, Ragga MC – explosive intense

KARISMA
21 year old, Yorkshire-born mixed-race girl – confident, unconventional

SAM
ageless feminine black guy – dry wit and wisdom

DANIEL
28 year old white Lawyer – home counties – old-fashioned – uptight – shy

KEVAN
21 year old white art student – middle-class, Northern – mouthy

ARRESTING OFFICER, JUDGE, PRISON OFFICER

The action takes place in East London today.

Pre-show – audience arrives to find...

Three hanging punch-bags. JJ in his space – EGGY and VENOM in theirs – kicking, punching, sweating, focused.

Lights down on EGGY and VENOM, light still up on JJ.

ORLANDO & JJ's flat

One Punch-bag. JJ is training.

SOUND: Key in the lock – front door opening then slamming.

JJ: Shit!

JJ darts to bathroom, pulling off his training wraps...

SOUND: Bathroom door slams.

...just as ORLANDO comes hurrying through, laden with shopping bags.

ORLANDO: Oh God, oh God, oh God, oh God...

Muttering anxiously as he scurries, ORLANDO pulls off his sarong, and struggling with a sandal, hops off to the bedroom.

Oh God, oh God, oh God, oh God...

SOUND: Bedroom door slams – bathroom door opens.

JJ bursts back in, chewing his toothbrush and struggling to spray under his arms whilst pulling on his top.

SOUND: Car horn.

JJ: Shit! Orly! We're late!

ORLANDO: (*Offstage.*) I know! Five minutes!

JJ hurries to the front door.

SOUND: Front door opening.

JJ: Five minutes, mate!

SOUND: Front door closes.

JJ: Orly! Where've you been? I've been texting you!

ORLANDO: I know! I'm sorry!

JJ: Did you fall asleep in the park again? Like that time I found you face down on your laptop?

ORLANDO: That was a year ago! First day of the first term when we first came to London! I was resting my eyes!

JJ: You were sleeping, Orly! In the park! You could have been mugged or raped or pissed on!

ORLANDO: Stop – I'm getting an erection! I've been shopping!

JJ: 'Shopping'? This is my big night.

ORLANDO: (*Offstage.*) I know!

JJ: This is the biggest Bashment event on the calendar, babe.

ORLANDO: (*Offstage.*) I know!

JJ: Do you know what DJs & MCs up and down the country would give to compete tonight?

ORLANDO: (*Offstage.*) I know!

JJ: Do you know what it means for a white boy from…

ORLANDO: (*Offstage.*) … 'Bristol to even get a sniff of this'? Yes, my lover, I know. Rude Boy have to 'come correc' innit'? and 't'row down on the 'Wheels of Steel'. Your face has to fit and your style has to blend. Which is why I've purchased…

ORLANDO enters in a loud hip-hop / ragga-ish outfit.

…this.

JJ: That?

ORLANDO: What's wrong with this?

JJ: (*Quickly.*) It's fine.

ORLANDO: What? This is dance-hall stylee! Okay, Rude Boy, bruk it down – from the feet up – What?

JJ: Well…

ORLANDO: Well?

JJ: Sandals, Orly?

ORLANDO: New butch sandals! Doc Marten Sandals! It's the painted toe-nails – I can clean 'em off in the cab.

JJ: It's a packed nightclub, babe. People dancing and stomping. You'll be crippled. You can wear my spare Timberlands.

ORLANDO: Fine. Timberlands. What about the rest of it?

JJ: Top's a bit tight.

ORLANDO: Yours is tighter.

JJ: Mine's guy tight. Yours is…

ORLANDO: … 'Gay tight'? (*Pulling at the top.*) Fine – we'll stretch it. – It's Gaultier, but we'll stretch it.

JJ: Orly, you asked.

ORLANDO: The trousers? Too tight?

JJ: Bit bright.

ORLANDO: Ragga is bright! (*Pulling CD from bag.*) I've
done my research! Ragga is fucking blinding! Look at
these lot – shirts in iridescent pink and retina-scorching
orange, red gold n' green string vests, Moschino
trousers pocked with glittering silver dollar signs, great
big gold necklaces and great big fuck-off diamante
earrings – they're fops, they're dandies, they're a gaggle
of fucking Miami drag-queens! Ragga is camp as fuck
and this outfit is fucking fierce!… What?

JJ: (*Taking a photo.*) It'sssss… cute… You're cute.

ORLANDO: But? Cute ain't required? Maybe I'm not
required then.

JJ: Orly, babe, we in't got time for this.

ORLANDO: I'm serious, JJ. I've blown a month's budget
on dressing like Beenie Man and I've minced out of the
bedroom looking like Queenie Man! I don't want to be
a liability.

JJ: You are not a liability.

ORLANDO: And I'm not deaf. I've listened to the music,
I've heard the lyrics and I know the score. Reggae
artists don't like bottymen…

JJ: … Battymen…

ORLANDO: … Or cha-cha men…

JJ: Chi-chi men. Not all of 'em.

ORLANDO: Just the ones that sing about it.

JJ: It's just music, Orly.

ORLANDO: Just music? Rude Boy, the day we first met you told me that hip-hop was your heart and ragga was the blood pumping round you. And suddenly, when you finally notice they're preaching that we don't have the right to fucking breathe, it's 'just music'? They're trying to tell us something, love. If being a white boy in the Dancehall is a hurdle to jump – being a gay boy is gonna be a fucking canyon. And when I'm around you're gay in great big pink neon lights – and The Music don't like it.

JJ: (*Stroking ORLANDO's cheek.*) Orly…

ORLANDO: Look at you, touching another man's face and staring into his eyes… You're a great big faggamuffin.

JJ: Orlando – My lover – It's…just…music. Yeah, it's a powerful thing. A river of rhythmic blood runs through it. It's the voice of struggle – it's the beat of freedom and infinite possibility. But it's still just Music. It in't perfect. It's like us, still growing, still learning – and to reach its massive potential it needs to face and be faced by its fear – Just like us. The Music needs this love – just like us. The Music needs the lyrics you inspire. The Music needs you. I'm gonna seize that DJ contest tonight – I'm gonna step up, claim our damn prize, thank my lover and walk out of there with you on my arm – and we're gonna change the world. Now let's fetch some Tims to protect those feet and catch that cab, what do you say?

ORLANDO: I say… Lyrics. I love you, Rude Boy.

ORLANDO puts on the Timberlands. JJ looks round at the clothes strewn along the ground – he smiles – he pulls out his digital camera and starts to photograph ORLANDO's trail.

Petrol station / EGGY & VENOM's flat

Two punch-bags – VENOM & EGGY box furiously.

JULIAN WOLFAVITZ WHITE FANG, macked out in raggamuffin threads is dialling as he enters and joins a queue formed by SAM and DANIEL. KARISMA at the till.

SOUND: phone.

Still wearing boxing gloves, EGGY manages to answer his . flip phone.

EGGY: You're late.

FANG: Eggy man! I'm at the service station down the corner!

EGGY: Congratulations.

FANG: I'm jus' in the queue, blood! Me reach in five! You lot set?

EGGY: (*Struggling to open a bottle of water.*) Mmm.

FANG: Both me other bredrens there, yeah? Venom, yeah?

EGGY: (*Gulping water.*) Mmm.

FANG: Is wha' you saying? Venom's there, yeah?

EGGY: (*Post-gulp breath.*) Haaaaahhh… Yup.

FANG: What about KKK?

EGGY: What about him?

FANG: Did he pitch up yet? Cheese and bread, man! Jus mek I speak to your cousin, yeah?

EGGY taps VENOM's shoulder and hands him the phone.

EGGY: Talk this Nigga off the roof, man.

VENOM tucks the phone into the crook of his neck as EGGY wanders off.

VENOM: Whaddup Nigga!

FANG: Is how you tell me 'whaddup' like you don't know what time it is?

VENOM: Why, what time is it?

FANG: Don't play, blood, don't play, you get me? I and I ain't in no mood, for real, blood. Pressure reach, blood – pressure reoocach! Jus' answer me, blood – did KKK pitch yet?

VENOM: You mean he ain't with you?

FANG: (*Closing his eyes.*) I'm taking a deep breath now, Venom, man – to beg you me brudda, yeah? Get you n' Eggy showered, shampooed, press' n' dress' by the time me reach, me bredren, please, me beseech, it's pas' nine!

EGGY returns with a pair of cold beers. Taking a beer, VENOM hands the phone back to EGGY.

This is our night, dread! This is the big Kahuna, you get me? Peoples dem a flock from far-flung corner a the country for this t'rowdown tonight and they ain't come to play, blood! You peoples need to scrape the crust out your eye and be at the door all alert and ready to chip and gone, ca' we pitch up late and it's over, end of! You hearing me, blood? You feeling me?

EGGY rolls the cold beer across his brow and under his arms.

Venom, you feeling me?

EGGY: Yeah, man, seen.

FANG: You lot! I ain't playing, Egg-Man! This shit is real!

EGGY: Yeah blood, Real blood, feel you.

At that moment, KKK bursts into the petrol station...

KKK: Yo! Sista! Gimme a Twix!

FANG: KKK located – back on track – ETA t'ree minutes – come correct to the kerb when I bell you, seen?

EGGY: Seen man, seen...

FANG: Is wha' y' wan'? Snicker or Mars?

EGGY: Caramac.

VENOM: Kit-Kat and Flake.

FANG: I spoil you lot.

Petrol station

SOUND: cash register.

FANG: Yo, K!

KKK: Yo, sista!

KARISMA looks around, 'you can't be addressing me' style.

How long you plannin'a blank a brudda for?

FANG: K, bwoy, we ain't got time for this, man.

KKK (*Still focused on KARISMA.*) ... What am I, black or summink?

KARISMA: See that there behind you? That orderly line of people stood patiently waiting? Here in civilisation we call that a queue.

FANG (*Stepping forward.*) Alright, sis, alright darling, let's keep things moving, yeah? That's a Twix, a Kit-Kat, a Flake and a Caramac.

KARISMA: That's Q and a U and an E and…

KKK: See, this here in front of you? This gleaming ebony proof that there is a God and he loves black women? We call this a Black Man. And Black Man don't deal in queues – you get me, sis? Black Man have stood in 'nuff lines since time, you get me? Bread-line – dole-queue lines, immigration lines and police identification line-up. Well, Black Man broke away, seen? Black Man don't stand in line no more for nuttin'! Black man just step, from the back of the bus to the front, so, 'cause he knows he can count on his brudda and sista them cutting him a break. Or ain't it like that where you come from, lil' lassie?

KARISMA: Sorry, I keep trying to catch a glimpse of this sister you keep talking to – or is she like your imaginary friend that only you can see?

KKK: Is who you a talk to so?

KARISMA: Dunno, mate, who the hell are you? Next!

SAM: I suppose that must be me.

KKK's head turns with the deadly slowness of a Terminator as SAM moves forward on delicate feet to stand behind him.

'Scuse me, brotha…

KKK: Damn. Shouldn't you be on top of some Christmas tree somewhere?

SAM: That position's reserved for fully qualified fairies – I'm just a trainee – working in the community to earn my wings. (*To KARISMA.*) That's pump number three, a pack of Juicyfruits, some Red Rizla and a pack of Marlboro Lights, please.

KKK: You ain't mean to tell me you're serving this pussyraas bitch before me?

KARISMA: No.

KKK: Hell no!

KARISMA: I'll not be serving anyone before you…

KKK: Step off, batty boy…

KARISMA: … 'Cause I'll not be serving you. Pump number three, pack of Juicyfruits, pack of Red Rizlas and pack of Marlboro Lights – that's sixteen pounds eighty-five pence please.

KKK and KARISMA speak simultaneously.

KKK: … Listen bitch and listen good yeah…

KARISMA: That's my name. Don't wear it out…

FANG: Okay, okay, ding ding, end of round one – everyone in their corner, yeah? Okay, Sis, what's your name, yeah?

KARISMA: Bitch'll do fine…

FANG: Sista, sistaaaa – help a brudda, out, yeah? Check me out trying to hang like Kofi Annan, trying to reunite the peoples, yeah? So, why doncha contribute to world peace, yeah and give us your name, yeah?

KARISMA: Karisma.

FANG: Now, that's a name. See how creative Nubian peoples can be? That's pure poetry, right there, fi real. Is your real name, yeah?

KARISMA: Yes.

FANG: Oh, sista gyal, you lucky still – you come from creative stock. My parents named me Julian, man – I mean, whassatabout? 'Julian'? Julian Wolfavitz – AKA White Fang, 'sup? (*Shaking her hand.*) See my man here christened Dijon Socrates Lawrence the third AKA inna da area as KKK – Krazy Kop Killa – Prob'ly you hearda 'im?

KARISMA: Actually, no.

FANG: Well, sista – fi sure you will. Inevitability in effec'. It's all about time, sis – Nature will take its course and soon, seen, ca' tonight my man here and him crew – the Ilford Illmanics, them a compete in the MC throwdown and mek I tell you as their promoter, manager, mentor what-have-you that said show is seized for real – prisoners taken   castle captured, declare a damn ceasefire. See, what you a deal wit' here is a lyrical landscaper ready to tag his own Sistine chapel – a fledgling legend on the edge of success and so he's just a lickle bit cranky, just a lickle bit wired. Ain't about you, sis, or this lickle chi-chi man standing here, it's about artistic temperament and the agony of genius, ca' all this Nubian warrior needs is just one itty-bitty lickle Twix to soothe his savage breast so the mojo will flow and another brother can rise. Contribute to world peace, sis – support the arts, Uplif' the race – and give the brudda a flippin' twix, yeah?

Pause.

KARISMA: Next.

SAM: Still me. (*Searching in a very girly back-pack.*) Do you take Switch?

KARISMA: When your lyrical landscaper comes up with a phrase deeper than Gimme a Twix – he can colour me impressed, alright? (*To SAM.*) Switch away darlin'...

Just as the card is about to change hands, KKK puts his hand over SAM's.

KKK: Yo. Sista. Give me a Twix.

DANIEL: Excuse me.

All turn to see DANIEL, standing in line.

Do you think you could take your hand off him?

KKK / WHITE FANG: Say what?

DANIEL: Sorry, that was rude of me – Do you think you could take your hand off him...please?

KKK: Who the fuck are you – his boyfriend?

DANIEL: Sadly not.

WHITE FANG: Damn raasclaat batty boys, man – they're fucking everywhere! Babylon a' crawlin'!

KKK: Nah, blood, He ain't gay, jus' posh. Ain't it, blue blood? You ain't a no gay pussyraas?

DANIEL: I prefer queer, actually. Well, I'm old fashioned. Can't bear to stand aside while a brute manhandles a beauty. Just have to 'step up' – I believe that's the phrase? – step up, speak up and ask you respectfully to take your hands off him, please.

KKK: You think I don't know what brute means? You think I don't know words and meanings? You think you can stand there and talk down like you so high and me so low? You drink spunk for breakfast up your dirty raas and you talk down to me? You don't know me. You ain't got no concept of me whatsoever. But what if I am just another ig'erant belligerent nigger n' I complete your picture of me and crush your bitch's paw in my fist like a biscuit? What if I fuck you both up and step over your bodies with my Twix n' gwan my way? What then?

DANIEL: I don't know. What then?

KKK: I'm gonna arx one more time – Yo…sista… Give me a Twix.

Pause.

KARISMA. Magic word?

Pause.

KKK: Please.

KARISMA produces a Twix – holds it out…

KKK produces a five pound note and holds it out to KARISMA. The Twix and cash change hands. KKK bites into the unopened Twix and strides out.

FANG: Keep the change, yeah?

FANG starts to leave just as KKK strides back in to stand burning in the doorway staring at KARISMA.

KKK: Think you're cute, innit? Think you got it all sorted – think you ain't ghetto. Just 'cause your upwardly-mobile nigger daddy found a white bitch to be his baby mama and you grew up talking like the enemy you think you ain't ghetto, innit? Well, when you marry your nice lickle white boy with his nice lickle white job and his nice lickle white house in nice lickle Whitetown and you take your nice lickle mulatto baby out in his nice lickle white pram and all the nice lickle white mums arx you how long you been his fucking nanny

you'll see just how cute you ain't and you'll know just
how ghetto you are. And when that moment reach and
you call your Gay Best Friend and he sends your call to
voicemail – think of this moment, yeah, and remember
– you coulda connected with a brudda. Someone coulda
had your back. You get me?... Sista?

*He walks out. After a moment, WHITE FANG walks straight
up to DANIEL, elbows him in the face and walks out.*

Bashment basement stage

*SOUND: Music blasting – bass pulsing – Lights
whirling...*

JJ: 'Ear me now! Judgement day reach and t'rough the
riddim me a' say creation a preach! Mek Man, woman
& pickney, let the beats them a teach – you leaaaarn!

> See me 'ere like a lily 'pon the water
> White fi true
> White fi true
> Take me down like a lamb to the slaughter
> White fi true
> White fi true
> Close your eyes, seen, and open your mind
> See me there without prejudice and lies
> Your soul brudda and your partner in crime
> Hear me soul in the flows of me Rhyme
> Like the soil and the silt from the shore of the
>   Nile River
> Dark fi true – Dark fi true
> Like the sweet sugar cane from heart of
>   Mudda Africa
> Dark fi true – Dark fi true
> Feel me now, me brudda
> Father, sister, mudda,
> Time fi chugga, chugga,

Dance the chugga chugga!
Whine it! Chugga Chugga Chugga!
Grine it! Chugga Chugga Chugga!

Share the humanity me bredren, share the love! For in the eyes of the Music, we are all African! Unity! Peace!

Bashment basement – Competitors' area

Buzzing, JJ goes to stand with ORLANDO, who hands him a can of Red Stripe as they try to hang casual.

ORLANDO: Oh – My – God, Rude-Boy! How proud am I?

JJ: Yeah? Was I cool?

ORLANDO: I don't know about cool. Seemed pretty fucking hot to me.

JJ: Orly…

ORLANDO: Well, what can I do? You know I'm helplessly horny when you chat Blackney like that!

JJ: Orly!

ORLANDO: I know! Seen! Be cool! I'm being cool! Can we hi-five? Is that cool?

They hi-five. ORLANDO swaggers as macho as he can muster.

Cool, geezer! …What?

JJ: (*Grinning.*) Nothing.

ORLANDO: I look funny.

JJ: You look great.

ORLANDO: But do I look straight? Do I pass?

JJ: I'm sorry, Orly.

ORLANDO: What? Is it the eyeliner? – I thought I'd got it all off!

JJ: Orly…

ORLANDO pulls out a tissue and rubs at his eyes.

ORLANDO: Fuck!

JJ: …Orly.

JJ reaches out and gently takes ORLANDO's hand away. They break contact, quickly looking round.

I'm sorry. This in't you. But I'll make it up to you, I swear.

ORLANDO: Yeah?

They smile.

JJ: Ohhh yeah… Soon as we get home.

ORLANDO: Oh God…

JJ: Soon as we reach yard, man!

ORLANDO: Oh God!

JJ: Before the door even close, man! You gon' see how a thug makes love, lickle English bwoy.

ORLANDO: Stop it JJ. These trousers in't that baggy.

JJ: Do you know how bad me wan' kiss you right now, lickle English?

ORLANDO: Actually… I think I do.

JJ: Wrap my arms roun' you…

ORLANDO: JJ…!

JJ: Wine and grine you… make you feel my lover's rock!

ORLANDO: (*Laughing…*) JJ! Why is that so bloody sexy?

JJ: 'Cause blackness is realness – and realness is sexy.

ORLANDO: So how come you ended up with the whitest boy on the planet this side of Prince Charles?

JJ: You ain't white, Orly. You're blinding.

JJ looks around, holds up his hand – they share another hi-five, this time lingering a moment, fingers entwining…

EGGY, VENOM, KKK and WHITE FANG come busting in. ORLANDO & JJ pull apart.

EGGY: Bo! Start the show! Niggas reach!

VENOM: Illmanics in da house! Mek the festivities commence!

EGGY: Where the Niggas at, man?

WHITE FANG: I dunno man, this is where them said congregate, yeah – lef' of stage innit?

KKK: Something ain't right, Bwoy, something ain't right… (*Up in JJ's face.*) What the fuck you lookin' at?

JJ: Whassup blood – MC KKK, yeah? MC Venom – MC Eggy, Illmanic crew! Boss man, boss man, feel your work, legends man, legends! (*Offering his hand to WHITE FANG.*) You the manager? Peace, blood.

WHITE FANG (*Giving JJ the hairy eyeball.*) I know you?

JJ: JJ.

Zero response.

They call me MC JJ. You guys here to check the show?

EGGY: We're here to win it – where's the organisers and alla dat?

JJ: Oh, they're probably up at the bar.

VENOM: Damn, bwoy, how black peoples come so lazy? Ain't no negro event ever start on time since the pyramids!

EGGY: For real.

JJ: Well, you know, this is the break.

Silence.

WHITE FANG: The break?

JJ: Before the second round?

VENOM: What the raas happened to the firs' round?

JJ: Firs' round done, man.

VENOM: Done?

JJ: Firs' round gone.

WHITE FANG: I'll fix it.

WHITE FANG exits.

EGGY: 'MC JJ'?

JJ: Seen, man.

EGGY: From where?

JJ: Bristol – West country boy.

EGGY: All the way to Eastside from West countryside, is it?

JJ: Innit. It's well cool to meet you, man, I love your work, Fi true. I feel that shit.

KKK: (*Looking at him darkly.*) You feel that shit?

JJ: (*Looks at him.*) Yeah, man.

KKK: You feel that shit?

JJ: Believe.

WHITE FANG returns.

EGGY: White fang! Whassuuuup!

VENOM: So, is wha' them say, man?

Silence.

KKK: Well?

WHITE FANG: (*Kissing his teeth.*) This system just corrup, man… Organisers them come like white man – fucking rigid! Them reckon first round done and gone.

VENOM: So, wha'? We miss a round?

WHITE FANG: We missed the whole thing, period. We bounced.

VENOM: 'Bounced'?

EGGY: 'Bounced'?

VENOM: You did stan' there and let them tell you we was bounced and never tell 'em nuttin' back?

WHITE FANG: What you want me 'a tell 'em, man? 'It's cause we're black'?

EGGY: 'Bounced'? The Illmanics is bounced? How can that be? How can it be that the Illmanics is bounced and the little white pig-fucker farm boy is t'rough? Eh? Country? How you pull that trick?

ORLANDO: He was on time?

47

All head snaps to ORLANDO.

JJ: … Orly…!

All heads snap to JJ Then back to ORLANDO.

KKK: And what the fuck is that?

JJ: That's Orlando. He's with me.

VENOM: 'With you'?

VENOM, EGGY & KKK exchange a look.

EGGY: Is wha' the fuck a gwan here, man?

WHITE FANG: So now we losing to a coupla chi-chi man?

VENOM: That's too Babylon even for me!

EGGY: Nah, man they ain't queer boys – not and be ahead of our game. That ain't even a possibility still, you get me?

VENOM: Too Babylon, man!

SOUND: We hear the competition COMPERE.

COMPERE: Round two commencing – could MC JJ please take the stage?

JJ looks at ORLANDO… The ILLMANICS watch them.

ORLANDO: I'll be fine.

JJ: I want you to stand by the edge of the stage – where you can see me, yeah? Right here, Yeah?

ORLANDO: JJ, I'll be fine.

EGGY: Yeah, blood, he'll be fine.

KKK: He's got us to take care of him, innit, blood?

COMPERE: Last call for MC JJ!

JJ: Right here, yeah? I'll be looking for you.

JJ steps onto the stage reluctantly… ORLANDO looks round at the ILLMANICS and smiles nervously. The ILLMANICS smile back broadly.

SAM's place

DANIEL sits in a bean-bag with frozen peas on his nose… SAM goes through a book of CDs…

SAM: I think this calls for Nina. How do you feel about Nina?

DANIEL: I'm not sure we've been introduced.

SAM: You'll love each other.

SOUND: Nina Simone – 'That's all I want from you'.

Meet Nina Simone, my heroine. Nina, meet…

DANIEL: … Daniel…

SAM: … Daniel… My hero.

DANIEL: Please to meet you, Miss Simone.

DANIEL hawks and spits blood into a blood-soaked tissue.

SAM: Let me look at that…

SAM dabs at DANIEL's nose, DANIELS hisses and winces…

I've not said thank you, have I? Gratitude is somewhat of a dying art. Once a maiden would've awarded her knight her favour to wear.

DANIEL: And he would henceforth wear her colours with pride. (*Pause.*) I'm rather liking this.

SAM: Really? That's impressively kinky.

DANIEL: I mean Miss Simone.

SAM: Oh, the Nina! Always good for what ails you.

They listen a moment…

Well – I think you're all bled out for now.

SAM takes the ice pack off to the kitchen.

I do like your flat. You're very creative.

SAM: And you're very diplomatic.

DANIEL: Seriously. I'm envious. Colour clearly doesn't scare you. My walls are all white with a hint of nicotine. Do you rent or buy?

SAM returns.

SAM: I squat. I'm a cluster of clichés I'm afraid. A slightly druggy, slightly draggy, dropout with an inadvertent tendency to draw drama like a magnet.

DANIEL: You know it wasn't your fault, don't you? That your people don't appreciate you. It must be even more disappointing for you, when it comes from your own, like that.

SAM: As opposed to when it comes from your own?

DANIEL: Well, you come to expect it from the white-trash element – The townies – the chavs…

SAM: … But never from the nice middle-class white boys. They just love the queers, don't they?

DANIEL: Trust me, I've no illusions regarding the middle-classes – but they don't go queerbashing on the streets

SAM: No, they go queer-bashing in the *Daily Mail* and the House of Lords. But the blacks – surely they should understand oppression, shouldn't they? After all they've been through.

DANIEL: Well… Shouldn't they?

SAM: After all, we're all on the same side, aren't we?

DANIEL: … Aren't we? Shouldn't we be?

SAM: In a world where two and two made four we would be.

DANIEL: And what does two and two make in this world?

SAM: A lynch mob. (*Peering at SAM's nose.*) I don't think it's broken.

DANIEL: I suspect it's black eyes by dawn, though.

SAM: Oh, I always wake up looking like a raccoon – but that's the danger of sleeping in cheap mascara for you. Well, maybe I won't wash tonight and in the morning we'll be a matching pair.

DANIEL looks back at SAM's shyly smiling face…

DANIEL: Oh, shit.

SAM: Oh dear. Do we hear another sorry coming over the hill?

DANIEL: I'm just not suited to this. One-night-stands – sex – dating. Truth be told I'm a bit of a theoretical queer. Strong on concept, lousy in practice. I'm great at cybersex, cruising, wham-bams, a quick tug and a toss. But kissing confuses me. Sharing the cigarette, pillow-

talk, love-tokens, dizzying romance, cosy domesticity
– having and holding – I get flustered.

SAM: And colour scares you?

DANIEL: It's not you. You are arrestingly lovely and
instantly intriguing and henceforth on the regular
occasions that I abuse myself in the lavatory at the
uninspiring major league law firm where I force myself
to work to advance my career, I shall invariably recall
the trembling excitement of sitting on this bean-bag in
your strange little burrow of a home – and smile and
weave florid fantasies around what could have been
if only I'd had the balls to ask you out. But if I fumble
through a clumsy attempt to actually connect with you
for real – I'll fuck it all up. And so – tragically – I cannot
stay. (*Getting to his feet.*) I feel like a deserter in time of
war. Who was it that said that we're forever responsible
for those whose lives we save?

SAM: The Apaches. And look what happened to them.

DANIEL starts to leave.

Wait.

*DANIEL halts. SAM pulls off a sweatband off his own wrist
and slips it onto DANIEL's.*

DANIEL: To treasure. Thank you.

DANIEL leaves – SAM watches him go.

Bashment basement stage

*ORLANDO watches from the edge of stage as JJ rocks the
mic.*

JJ: Hear me now! Second round reach!

White boy come again fe snatch the crown!

Whine it! Chugga Chugga Chugga!
Grine it! Chugga Chugga Chugga!

The ILLMANICS storm the stage.

VENOM: Niggas reeeeach!

EGGY: Now 'ear dis, now 'ear dis… this is not a tes' say
this is not a drill!

KKK: This dancehall a requisition by the People dem
Liberation Army known 'pon the street as The Illmanic
Crew.

Mc VENOM: Resistance is futile repeat Resistance is futile
– is time fe surrender!

EGGY: T'row up your 'and muthafuckas and assume the
position!

VENOM: Alla my Niggas at the MC Trow-down
Alla my homies outta Brixton Lockdown!
Trow them gats in the air firing one round
Shoutin'
Where my niggas at?

ILLMANICS: Yo! Where my Illmanics?

EGGY: My sweet bitches from the Barking Area!
My sweet hunnies all from Illford, see 'em dere?
Tear out them weave from their scalp in hysteria
screamin'
Where my niggas at?

ILLMANICS: Yo! Where my Illmanics?
Niggas reach! East London!

KKK: Looking cris, looking down,
come fe claim the black crown

ILLMANICS: Niggas reach! East London!

KKK: See how me dress to impress
     How me step wid'out stress?

ILLMANICS: Niggas reach – East London!

KKK: Is a black man ting – to look this fine a' take a
     brudda time, you get me? Make them white boys reach
     early and nasty up the place – black man dress to
     represent the race!

ILLMANICS: Niggaaaaaas reeaaaaach!

JJ: Yo yo yo… Hol' on, yeah, hol' on…

> Scuse me, brudda,
> If you don't mind,
> this is my moment,
> This is my time…
> Sorry blood, yeah?
> Nuff respect
> But this is my stage,
> And JJ's in effec'
> How come Johnny Come Lately you say only white
>   boys reach early fi true?
> When rocking the house is a sea of black faces all
>   reach in dis place before you?
> A wha' G'wan?
> Ain't your mamma raise you to know that it's rude
>   to intrude? A Wha' Gwan?
> Ain't your papa tell you that every ting in the world
>   ain' all about you?
> A wha' gwan?
> All your plans spannered
> So you forget your manners
> And now you step to a brother like you fixing fi
>   fight?
> Something ain't right, bwoy, Something ain't right!

EGGY: First t'ing Muthafucka, you bes' start address me as
    mister
    'cause this nigga he ain't your brother no way
    and you ain't my sister
    Make me laugh how you t'ink you stan' 'pon this
    stage like you some kind of wheel, star…
    When your hairy-ass bitch has a dick for a clit 'cause
    your gyal is a geezer!

MC VENOM: But wait, dread, my boy here, he can't be a
    homo, me na understand!
    For the dude to be batty, my nigga, he'd have to be
    screwing a man!
    Yeah, I know his lickle bitch needs a shampoo and
    shave and he must be out of his mind…
    but loving a dog – well it might be a sin,
    But technically it ain't a crime

KKK: Did you really think, wigga to real nigga, you could
    pull wool over this brutha's eyes?
    That you and your pussy-raas punk boy could mug
    up the negroes and take home the prize?
    If you tink you can fuck with this black man then
    white boy your cornrows them fix up too tight
    Just do what you do best and ben' over bitch, 'cause
    you really getting fucked tonight!

ILLMANICS: A wha' g'wan?

KKK: Alla dem so-call lyrical gangstas
    and bruk-ass MC pretender –

ILLMANICS: A wha' g'wan?

KKK: Alla dem nasty raas chi-chi men, batty bwoy nature
    offender

ILLMANICS: A wha' g'wan?

KKK: Them swallow man's dick

Then wan fi spit lyrics
Then they step to a brotha like them fixing fi fight?

ILLMANICS: Something ain't right, bwoy,
Something ain't right!

JJ: So, the word's on the street, yo
The homie's a homo,
Illmanics feel sick
But what am I made of
That you're so afraid of
A guy who likes dick?
Now could it be what's really freaking you out is
    your ass gettin' kicked?
'Cause this faggot's proud to say I never found me a
    pussyrass I couldn't lick

Or maybe it's just that the babe on my arm is way
    finer than you'll ever own
Yeah, actually blood, if you all are such studs –
how come Mister Lover's alone?

Could it be being bigoted don't make you blacker
It just makes you fucked up and sad?
Or what's messing with your head the fact that last
    night dread, I fucked both your mum and dad?
A wha' gwan?
What the big deal who I fuck with If I ain't fucking
    with you?
A wha' g'wan?
Is that what's really bugging you boys?
Are you hungry for a lickle piece of JJ too?
A' wha' g'wan?
Should I be flattered?
Are your hopes shattered?
Is that why you step to a brother inciting a fight?
Something ain't right, bwoy, Something ain't right!

ALL: A Wha' Gwan – A Wha' Gwan – A Wha' Gwan – A Wha' Gwan – A Wha' Gwan – A Wha' Gwan – A Wha' Gwan – A Wha' Gwan – A Wha' Gwan?
…Is Wha' Gwan?

COMPERE: Illmanics – your disqualification stands – Will the Illmanics please leave the stage – your disqualification stands…

The ILLMANICS slink off the stage…

T'ank you! MC JJ commence!

Bashment basement / Halls of residence

ORLANDO & KEVAN on their mobiles

ORLANDO: Hey, Kevin.

KEVAN: Kevan.

ORLANDO: Kevin's a perfectly good name.

KEVAN: It's yours if you want it – I'm sure it'll suit you. I, meanwhile will be answering to the name Kevan.

ORLANDO: Start again, shall we? Hey Kevan.

KEVAN: Hey yourself. So, you're still there?

ORLANDO: Somehow, yes.

KEVAN: Surrounded by black blokes in string vests, all rapping about the size of their dicks – God, I hate you.

ORLANDO: Take a ticket and get in line.

KEVAN: They giving you attitude are they? Staring at you with angry burning hostile eyes?

ORLANDO: (*Drily.*) Stop! I'm getting an erection.

KEVAN: I shouldn't worry too much. No-one'll notice your little white Somerset mushroom in that jungle of tree trunks.

ORLANDO: Kevan…

KEVAN: Sorry, I get carried away.

ORLANDO: They are sexy though – in a scary way.

KEVAN: The best kind of sexy. Is loverboy about to win?

ORLANDO: Well, I think he should.

KEVAN: But then you would – ooh, Rhyme! I got skillz! With a z! Maybe I should come down there! Orlando, mate…

ORLANDO: Yeah?

KEVAN: Do you want me to come down there?

ORLANDO: I'm fine. Don't want to overrun the place. That's the trouble with you honkies – Don't know when you're not welcome.

KEVAN: 'Honkies'? Do people still stay that?

ORLANDO: Probably. This is not the most politically correct environment. If I hear the n-word one more time…

KEVAN: The 'n' word'? Forgive me, I don't speak Coy. Do you mean Nigga?

ORLANDO: Kevan!

KEVAN: With an 'a'! It's okay with an 'a' at the end. That's just keeping it real. You just said yourself they're all saying it.

ORLANDO: Well, I can't get used to it, I'm sorry. Everytime I hear the word nigger I just hear the e-r.

KEVAN: Ooops! Said it! And you've not been nicked by the PC police.

ORLANDO: I know it's me that's terminally unhip – they bandy it about round the place like it's nothing – there's a Nigga in every sentence.

KKK, VENOM, EGGY & WHITE FANG appear. ORLANDO does not see them.

Honestly! it's Nigga this and Nigga that… It makes me clench. I'm clenching right now as we speak.

KEVAN: Well, don't give yourself contractions.

ORLANDO: Well, I can't be bandying words with you I've got a man to watch! Laters!

KEVAN: Peace out!

ORLANDO: Innit!

They hang up. ORLANDO turns to find hisself face to face with the ILLMANIC CREW.

EGGY: 'Nigger'? Did I hear you say 'Nigger'?

ORLANDO: With an 'a' – Nigga with an 'a' – Anyway, I was just saying how I hate that word.

EGGY: How you hate Niggas?

ORLANDO: The word. I hate the word. I love Niggas – black people – I'm from an estate when it was like eighty per cent black. I don't hate anyone. We are all Africans.

The ILLMANICS looks at one another then bust out laughing.

EGGY: You just too funny, brudda man.

VENOM: Ah, leave him man…he's just a lickle chi-chi man. Make him gwan with him nasty self, yeah?

EGGY: Oh man, now you're just being scandalous and slanderous. How can an African be a chi-chi man? That just ain't logical.

EGGY slips an arm round ORLANDO's shoulders.

How can a righteous, conscious god-fearing, African man be a batty boy? Ain't no way. You ain't no batty boy, is it, Orlando, my nigga? You ain't dutty so? Is it?

MC VENOM: Man, leave him, he's cool. You're cool, innit, blood?

EGGY's arms tightens round ORLANDO's shoulders.

EGGY: 'Course he's cool. He ain't gonna come inna dis place and stand up in our face and bring nasty batty boy business inna di space…is it? Nah, man – It's you what ain't cool – bad-mouthing me bredren like him gay. Just wrong, innit, blood? You don't take dick do you, blood? Go on, put this fool straight – You ain't no dutty raas batty boy.

KKK: It's okay, bredren. You're among fambly, now. You ain't gotta be politically correc'. Just say it yeah, and mek we let you gwan your way, yeah?

EGGY's arms tightens round ORLANDO's neck.

VENOM: Just tell him you ain't a batty, yeah, dread, and he'll let you go.

EGGY: You know it, cuz! He's right, blood, just tell me you ain't gay an' dat and you can go, yeah? You alright, blood? I ain't choking you am I?

WHITE FANG: He can't say it 'cause he's a queer. Innit? White boy? You are a dutty raas pussyraas, bloodclaat queer – Innit, Chi-chi man? Innit?

ORLANDO: Yes.

Pause

KKK: Is wha' you say? Yes? You said yes?

ORLANDO: Yes.

WHITE FANG: And every night you suck that wigga wannabe's cock. Innit? And you love it, innit? You fucking love it. SAY IT! You fucking love it!

ORLANDO: I… Love…him.

The ILLMANICS look at one another.

VENOM: Love him? You fucking Love him? A man? A bloke? A geezer? Fucking Love?

KKK: Now, ain't that a fucking bitch?

WHITE FANG: Nah, man…

WHITE FANG punches ORLANDO in the face.

WHITE FANG / EGGY / KKK: That's a fucking bitch!

Stunned, ORLANDO slumps into EGGY's arms. KKK back-hands him and sends him spinning into the centre of the stage. The beating continues, mimed, without any actual contact.

KKK: Feel that shit!

EGGY head-butts ORLANDO.

EGGY: Suck that, bitch!

VENOM: Oh, man, why you lot have to go and do that for? Now it's gotta be on for real – And we all gotta be in it! Aww, shit!

VENOM punches ORLANDO in the back of the head. ORLANDO drops to his knees.

(*Flexing his sore hand…*) … Shit!

The ILLMANICS take turns to kick and stamp on ORLANDO relentlessly until he lies on the ground in a pool of red.

KKK: Pussy.

KKK exits.

EGGY: Faggot.

EGGY exits.

WHITE FANG: Queer.

WHITE FANG exits.

VENOM looks down at ORLANDO bleeding…

VENOM: Why'd you have to go and bring Love into it, man?

VENOM exits.

We hear the crowd roar. JJ runs in holding his mic.

JJ: Yeah, man! Orly? Where the fuck were you?

JJ sees ORLANDO.

(*A whisper.*) Orly?

JJ drops the mic – BOOM – the SOUND FX echoes as he runs to ORLANDO.

Orly?

Lifting ORLANDO's face, JJ is confronted by a mask of blood.

Orly! Oh no!

He pulls out his mobile phone and tries to switch it on, but his hand is shaking too much...

Oh fuck! Oh no! No, no, no..

JJ struggles to pick ORLANDO up.

Hold onto me, Orly, I've got you... Shit!

JJ slips in the blood, almost dropping ORLANDO.

Orly! I'm sorry, I've got you, I got you baby... I've got you...

JJ carries ORLANDO out – leaving red footsteps.

Petrol station / EGGY & VENOM's flat

SOUND: Till.

KARISMA is working behind the till – KKK bursts in and starts pacing. She watches him, warily.

EGGY, VENOM & WHITE FANG come running in the flat.

EGGY / VENOM / WHITE FANG: Yeh man!

KKK: Yo, sista – gimme a twix, yeah – please?

KARISMA hands KKK a Twix. He unwraps it. He bites it. He chews...

VENOM & EGGY snatch up their PlayStation consoles and start to play...

SOUND: Video game.

VENOM: Yeah baby yeah baby yeah baby, yeahhhhhh!

EGGY throws down his console.

EGGY: Shit, man!

WHITE FANG hands EGGY & VENOM a beer each.

Stupid fucking queer, man…

WHITE FANG: Stupid fucking batty man…

WHITE FANG, EGGY AND VENOM drink.

KARISMA: He was white.

KKK: What?

KARISMA: My dad. Was white. My mum was the black one. He worked in a tannery – skinning sheep. He was not a nigga. Nor was she – Nor am I.

KKK: 'Was'?

KARISMA looks blankly puzzled.

'He was'? 'She was'?

KARISMA: When they were alive.

KKK lunges at KARISMA – kisses her on the lips.

FANG: You lot – I'm off home, yeah?

KKK: (*Breaking off the kiss.*) See you round, yeah?

As WHITE FANG & KKK heads towards their prospective doors they hear…

SOUND: Police siren.

EGGY, VENOM, WHITE FANG & KKK all stop in their tracks.

Police station / holding cell

VENOM, EGGY, WHITE FANG & KKK in a small room.
They hold white cards.

KKK: Fuck – this – shit – man.

WHITE FANG: We'll be cool if we stick together, bredren.

KKK: Fuck this shit.

WHITE FANG: It's all about unity, bredren.

VENOM: What you tell 'em man?

EGGY: Nuttin'.

VENOM: Same here.

EGGY: Didn't see nuttin', didn't hear nuttin', don't know nuttin', ain't got nuttin' to say.

WHITE FANG: Four bredren, one story. Safe.

EGGY: Nuttin'. (*Raises his voice.*) The truth!

KKK: Fuck 'em.

SOUND: Voice over speaker system.

VOICE: Numbers two, five, six and eight stand in line please…

They look at their cards… They are numbered 2, 5, 6 and 8.

KKK: (*Kissing his teeth.*) Fuck you.

VENOM: That's us.

KKK: Fuck that.

VENOM, WHITE FANG & EGGY get in line.

And fuck you lot. Black man don't stand in line for no-one!

VOICE: Number six...

KKK: Fuck off.

VOICE: Number six...

KKK gets in line.

Hold your cards in front of you...

A curtain of light comes up on the ILLMANICS, causing them to squint slightly.

Turn to your left...

ILLMANICS turn to face their left...

...and now right...

ILLMANICS turn to face their right.

And front once more please...

ILLMANICS turn front.

Light up on JJ, his clothes covered in blood.

JJ: Number two, number five, number six and number eight.

The lights on the ILLMANICS return to normal.

VENOM: Well, that's us fucking kippered ain't it?

EGGY: Shut up – he weren't there – we weren't there – no eye-witnesses, no ID. Nobody knows nothing. You get me?

KKK: This is bullshit.

VOICE: Julian Wolfavitz – step forward.

WHITE FANG: Fuck! They mean me. (*Stepping forward.*) Yeah?

VOICE: Room three please.

WHITE FANG: You lot. Unity, yeah?

They touch fists.

Leave it wi' me, yeah? I'll fix this.

FANG goes off.

SOUND: Door closing.

KKK: This is beyond bullshit.

VOICE: Duran Hunter, please step forward.

EGGY steps forward.

EGGY: This gonna take long? My mum's making curried goat and pigfoot this evening.

VOICE: Show your palms, please…

EGGY shows his hands.

EGGY: And you know she don't like to reheat.

LIGHT FX: Photo flash.

VOICE: Turn the hands over, please…

EGGY turns his hands over…

LIGHT FX: Photo flash.

VOICE: Thank you. Step back.

EGGY: Pleasure working with you.

VOICE: Marquis Campbell, please remove your shoes.

VENOM quickly removes his shoes.

Hold them out, soles facing up…

VENOM does this.

LIGHT FX: Three photo flashes in succession.

VOICE: Thank you.

Dijon Socrates Lawrence…

KKK: … The third – and I ain't doing shit!

SOUND: Door opening.

WHITE FANG hurries back in. Pale. The others look at him.

VENOM: What man? What?

WHITE FANG: Fucking Bablyon got DNA, bredren.

VENOM: They got science? Shit man!

Light change.

Interview room

SOUND: Door opening.

DANIEL enters holding four case histories, he shakes each ILLMANIC by hand.

DANIEL: Mr Hunter, Mr Campbell, Mr Wolfavitz, Mr Lawrence.

EGGY: And who the fuck are you?

DANIEL: Daniel Pearl. I'm your solicitor.

EGGY: Excuse me?

DANIEL: I've been assigned by legal aid to defend your case.

WHITE FANG: You're fired.

DANIEL looks at them.

DANIEL: Well, that was nice and quick.

WHITE FANG: Tell 'em to send a brutha in, a'ight? And make him straight while you're at it.

DANIEL: 'Make him straight…' Interesting…

DANIEL turns to go – EGGY, VENOM, KKK jump in his path.

EGGY: } { Wait wait wait, brutha, yeah?

KKK: } { Where you going, Brudda man, no need to be so sensitive, yeah?

VENOM: My Nigga here jus' trippin'. We need us a lawyer, man – Fang, man, what the fuck?

EGGY: How you gonna be dissing our only key to the gate, bruv?

WHITE FANG: He's redundant, man – muthafucka pure chi-chi!

VENOM, EGGY & KKK check out DANIEL.

KKK: How you know him chi-chi? You shagged him or what?

WHITE FANG: Too much chronic blunt your faculty fi memory, blood – you don't recognise him?

KKK looks at DANIEL.

KKK: They all look the same to me, blood, know what I'm saying?

WHITE FANG (*Mimic.*) 'I prefer queer, actually.'

KKK: Damn… For real?

WHITE FANG: For real!

EGGY: Yo! 'this a private conversation or can any Nigga join in?

WHITE FANG: We had an altercation with my man here and he himself reckons in public before witness dem that he is queer as a low-alcohol beer.

EGGY: A 'true?

WHITE FANG: How's a battyman gonna defend this case and not sell us down the fucking river? I may be a freak, but I ain't a fool, you get me?

EGGY: This true? You a battyman?

DANIEL: Well… I do prefer queer.

EGGY: Fuck's sake, man! Ain't nobody got no shame no more? Gwan! Gone! And tell 'em sen' a righteous Nigga up in here lickety-split, yeah?

DANIEL: Ah.

ILLMANICS: What?

DANIEL: That may prove irksome. I'm afraid there's only one heterosexual black man on legal aid in this catchment area – and he's snowed under with cases for a least a year.

VENOM: One black man? Man, where all the other triflin' lazy Niggas at?

DANIEL: All poached, every last one. Black solicitors are all the rage in the trendiest chambers currently. Ramsey might have space – Asian, plucks his eyebrows and calls everyone sista, very popular, but he might squeeze you in – There's a couple of black women – I think one of them might be straight or at least bisexual – would you like me to make enquiries?

WHITE FANG: So why ain't you booked up? You the dregs or what?

DANIEL: Ah – I am that rare breed – the bright-eyed bushy-tailed and brilliant socially conscious lawyer, freshly defected to legal aid in an attempt to satiate my white liberal guilt – Still principled enough to present your case with utmost commitment to the rule of law without personal prejudice. However, as you are so sure that a heterosexual black lawyer will be more sympathetic to your position – I must humbly bow to your collective decision. Good day, gentlemen.

DANIEL is about to hit the door.

VENOM: He called us Niggers.

DANIEL stops.

Alla us. He called us all niggers…

KKK: … We over-reacted, but he provoked us…

WHITE FANG: … And we're really, really sorry.

Courtroom

SOUND: Voice over speaker system.

VOICE: Let the accused stand…

The ILLMANICS face front.

Taking into consideration that three of the four perpetrators of this deed have no previous recorded convictions – along with your claim that the recipient of your attack provoked you by first mistaking you for drug-dealers and then subjecting you to a torrent of appalling racist abuse, I hereby accept your eleventh-hour plea bargain of guilty to the lesser crime of Actual Bodily Harm and I hereby sentence Hunter, Campbell and Socrates to two years in Her Majesty's Prison. As for you, Wolfavitz, I have taken into additional consideration the submission from your solicitor that considering your background and education, this situation was not typical of your previous character and that you were to a great extent playing a naïve game of follow-my-leader. You are sentenced to eighteen months. Bailiff take them down.

SOUND: Banging gavel.

VOICE: Stay in line. Step forward.

The ILLMANICS step forward.

Remove all your clothing except your underwear. Rule number one. You will not speak in the hallways – you will not speak in the showers – you will not speak unless in your cells, at meals or in the recreation areas – in fact no-one will speak unless spoken to and given permission to reply. Is rule number one understood?

By now in their underwear, the ILLMANICS nod.

Bend forward…

The ILLMANICS bend forward.

Lower your shorts.

As they start to lower their shorts…

Blackout.

ORLANDO & JJ's flat

JJ is sorting through the piles of clothes on the floor and putting them into a laundry basket.

SOUND: Doorbell.

JJ pulls out a knife that's hidden in the laundry...he approaches the door.

JJ: Who the fuck's that?

KEVAN: JJ? It's only me!

Hiding the knife, JJ opens the door.

SOUND: Two locks opening and a bolt being drawn back.

KEVAN enters holding up a newspaper.

Evening paper. Massive editorial – page of letters and emails. The nation up in arms.

KEVAN puts the paper on the laundry. JJ takes the laundry out without reading it...

Most reckon it should've been attempted murder and they should be serving life. Apparently 'cause they've already served ten months on remand, they'll be out in like six months with tags on their ankles. Mental. Who'd have thought it? The whole nation on the side of a couple of dirty queers – 'ccpt for one fucked-up old judge. Is Orly about? I brought his favourite beer.

JJ: Orly's asleep.

KEVAN: Oh. Sorry. (*Putting the beers back in the bag...*) ... Sorry...you want me to fuck off... Sorry...

JJ: (*Stopping him.*) You know what? Let's forget sorry. (*Taking the beers from the bag.*) Sorry's all used up. (*Hands a beer to KEVAN.*) Fuck sorry.

KEVAN: Fuck sorry.

They open their beers – they drink.

And when Orly's ready, he'll be ready. Just tell him nobody cares how he looks, okay? He can never be anything but beautiful. Anyway. Fuck sorry.

He drinks.

Do you think maybe you should have been there?

JJ: Mmm?

KEVAN: For the sentencing. Like made a special appeal to the Judge or something? I dunno. Forget it.

JJ: Orlando was coming home that day. I in't never leaving him alone again. Shit, yeah, probably should have been there… I in't never where I should be.

KEVAN: You were with Orly. Fuck sorry, yeah?

JJ: Fuck sorry.

They drink. ORLANDO calls from offstage…

ORLANDO: (*Offstage.*) JJ…?

JJ: (*Jumping up.*) Orly?

ORLANDO wanders in, dressed for bed…

ORLANDO: JJ!

JJ: I'm here, Orly babe, you can go back to bed! What you doing up again so soon?

ORLANDO: I had another nightmare…

JJ: Ohhh, baby…it's okay…

ORLANDO: I dreamed that my head was ice-cream and you was an Alstation…

JJ: …let's get you back to bed, yeah..?

ORLANDO: … And you kept licking my face and swallowing me!

JJ: (*Hugging ORLANDO, laughing despite himself.*) Orly!

ORLANDO: Bit by bit, my ears, my eyes, my eyebrows, my nose – I was a dog's dinner!

JJ: (*Rocking ORLANDO in his arms.*) Orly, Orly, Orly, silly Orly. It was just a dream. This is real. See, I'm me and you're you – You in't ice-cream, Orly, and I in't a dog – We're real.

A puddle of pee spreads round ORLANDO's feet…

Oh, Orly!

ORLANDO: (*Super innocent.*) What?

JJ nips off.

JJ: You know what! We've discussed this!

JJ Comes back with rubber gloves and a rag to mop the floor… ORLANDO spots KEVAN staring in shock.

ORLANDO: Keevie?

KEVAN: Hey you.

ORLANDO throws his arms round KEVAN, kisses, hugs and rocks him.

ORLANDO: Keevie, Keevie, Keevie… I've missed you, missed you, missed you. Where you flippin' been, man?

KEVAN: Missing you.

ORLANDO: I'm sorry, Keevie – I've been sick. I weren't allowed to come to school for ages and ages – But I'm nearly better now – I just have to take my headache pills and I'm cool. Oh, my Gosh! JJ! Can Kevan stay?

JJ: Kevan doesn't want to stay, silly, he's got things to do.

ORLANDO: Please, please, please! He can sleep in our bed, there's loads of room! Can he, can he, please?

JJ: Kevan, do you want to stay?

KEVAN: Sure.

ORLANDO: Yeaaahhh! I'll find my spare pyjamas!

ORLANDO runs out. JJ looks at KEVAN.

JJ: You okay?

KEVAN: You must hate them so much.

JJ starts to wrap his hands to box.

KEVAN: Not all of them, just the ones who are like them. The ghettoey ones.

JJ: This didn't happen cause they were black, mate.

KEVAN: Maybe not. But that's why they're getting away with it, isn't it? That's what was behind the judge's ruling. In the end you should have known how they'd react to a pair of batty boys. So it's your fault. They're not supposed to know better and you are.

JJ: Kevan, we can't think like this, man.

KEVAN: Can't we? Why can't we? Why can they? They're allowed to feel what they like because they're still recovering from slavery, is that it? We're not slave-owners. We're not racists. But does that mean we have to be fucking punch-bags just 'cause we're liberal white queers? Okay – they don't have to love us back but do they have to hate us?

JJ starts boxing with the punchbag...

JJ: Kevan, One of them was white.

KEVAN: He was white once he got to court – but when he was stamping your lover's brains out, what colour was he trying to be, then? It's all so fucked up and us letting 'em get away with this just fucks it up all the more. This feeling, man...what are we supposed to do with it?

JJ: I don't know. You sure you can handle staying the night, man? I know what Orlando means to you.

KEVAN: You mean I've always been a little bit in love with him.

JJ: It's cool. Who wouldn't be?

KEVAN: It's was never just Orlando. It was you and Orlando. Orlando and you. I was in love with the idea of you. What you stood for. You were Orly and JJ.

JJ: We're still Orly and JJ.

KEVAN: That's not Orly, though is it?

JJ: Don't be fooled, mate. He's lost a few years, but it's Orly, alright.

KEVAN: So, you're gonna still live together?

JJ: Orly and JJ for ever.

KEVAN: Are you really ready to be someone's dad for ever? What about his parents? Don't they want him with them? You have told 'em?

JJ: His mum put the phone down as soon as she heard my voice. I'm the Satan who lured her boy to Sodom.

77

KEVAN: Jesus, what's wrong with people?

JJ: People hate queers. Even nice white people. I should write and thank her. Imagine if she had wanted him back? I couldn't handle losing Orly entirely, man – It'd fucking fry me.

KEVAN: And what about sex?

JJ keeps punching…

You're twenty, JJ. Orly's – what, seven, now?

JJ: He's still beautiful. You said it yourself, he can never be anything but.

KEVAN: But you can't make love to a child, mate.

JJ: I know. But this my life. Orly and JJ.

ORLANDO: Keevie!

JJ: He's coming! (*To KEVAN.*) I'll catch you up, mate, okay?

KEVAN: Okay.

KEVAN goes into the bedroom – JJ batters away at the punchbag – his punches underscoring the next scene…

Prison block

EGGY in one cell, VENOM in another. Both lying on their bunks.

EGGY: Yo! V! V, man!

VENOM: Eggy? Whattup?

EGGY: Whattup you, cuz? Been calling you. Never seen you in the yard this morning. You cool?

VENOM: I'm cool, cuz. They just changed my recreation shift.

EGGY: Bastards! Sorry man. I tried to get us in the same cell and that. Babylon just cold.

VENOM: Cold, man! They took my cross, you know that?

EGGY: MUTHAFUCKAS!

VENOM: Eggy man, ain't you gonna wake your cellmate and that?

EGGY: My cellmate's well sleeping. Can't you hear him snoring? He's like a Hoover! Listen!

VENOM listens – EGGY makes snoring sounds… VENOM laughs.

VENOM: Crazy black bastard.

EGGY: How's your cell mate?

VENOM: Gone.

EGGY: Gone? You on your own?

VENOM: He's dead, man.

EGGY: Dead?

VENOM: Suicide, man. Woke up this morning and my man was just hanging there.

EGGY: What, by the neck? Shit man, and you never hear nuttin'?

VENOM: He was always quiet, man. Kind of a ghost even before he passed, I s'pose.

EGGY: Damn. So, you cool sleeping in that same cell n' that?

VENOM: Ah, Nigga, I'm strong, don't worry about it, still. I ain't the one killed hisself, is it? (*looks around.*) I dunno – bwoy, you see some things tho, in this life, ain't it?

EGGY: For real, cuz.

VENOM: How the fuck did we end up like this, cuz? How'd we end up here? Caught up in all this ragga business? We ain't even Jamaicans, man. Always trying to keep up with the Windians man. Ain't we the real Africans, though? It all started with us and here's us trying to hang – straining to chat like them from their tiny island. It's all wrong-side up, man.

EGGY: Don't do that, man. We never do that.

VENOM: Do what?

EGGY: We don't turn on our own. Every black man is a brother.

VENOM: What about coppers? And queers?

EGGY: They forfeit their blackness.

VENOM: And it's in the bible ain't it? Thou shalt not… Summink… I don't know, man, I swear…

EGGY: For real, cuz… Marquis, man, I'm sorry you ain't in with me, yeah? I ain't saying you're soft – I just wish… anyway, we just have to be strong and hold on – we ain't here for ever. We can come through.

VENOM: Yeah, man, we can come through.

EGGY: Stay strong, African man.

VENOM: Stay strong… Come through…

ORLANDO & JJ's flat

JJ goes over to pile of large-format photos and lays them out on the ground, overlapping the prints to complete a collage of ORLANDO's sleeping naked body. JJ lays down and, with an arm and leg draped over pictures of sleeping ORLANDO, closes his eyes…

INTERVAL.

Prison interview room

EGGY waiting.

SOUND: Door opening.

Enter VENOM.

VENOM: Whattup my bredren!

EGGY: Cuz! Still ugly!

They go into an elaborate handshake and bump a shoulder.

Bwoy, how you get skinny so?

VENOM (*Mimes toking.*) Ganja diet, innit?

EGGY: Bwoy bad! Staying lean, stayin' mean!

SOUND: Door opening.

WHITE FANG enters – he has a black eye.

EGGY / VENOM: My Nigga!

WHITE FANG: My boyz!!

They go into an elaborate three-way handshake.

EGGY: How's the runnins over in C wing? You some buff
Nigga's bitch, yet?

WHITE FANG: Yo, fuck you and the dick you rode in on,
ai'ight? I'm in a cell of four white muthafuckers, man.

EGGY: Aw, now Nigga, that ain't right!

WHITE FANG: You feelin' my pain?

VENOM: Jus' wrong, bro! Is them do that to that to your
face, blood?

WHITE FANG: They see me come in with you lot and they had a problem. I had to regulate innit? S'all under control.

SOUND: Door opening.

KKK enters.

KKK: Black peopllllllles!

VENOM / EGGY / WHITE FANG: Negroooooo!

They exchange a labyrinthine four-way handshake…

EGGY: Reunioooon!

VENOM: Illmanics in the houuuuuse!

WHITE FANG: Duck – and – cover! Drop and roll!

KKK: Fuck all that, man.

VENOM: Yeak, fuck alla dat, man – Fang, me bredren, is wha' the plan?

WHITE FANG: Plan, blood?

VENOM: For the appeal or whatever – it ain't you what arrange this rendezvous?

KKK & VENOM look at one another.

KKK: He don't know?

EGGY: V, man, you don't know?

SOUND: Door opening.

They all look round. JJ enters.

VENOM: Awww man! You gotta be fuckin' kiddin' me!

WHITE FANG: Welcome to 'Meet the victim'!

VENOM: You know what, fuck this, man.

EGGY: You heard the man. What you got to say, Country?

JJ pulls up a chair. He sits and looks at them.

VENOM: Ain't what he wants to say, man. It's what he wants to hear.

EGGY: Wha' y' wanna hear, wigga boy? Apologies? Want us to break down in tears and beg for forgiveness? Hang our heads in shame? You wan' see Niggas on their knees?

WHITE FANG: He wants us to turn back time and cure his bitch, innit?

EGGY: Is it? Jonesin' for your butt boy?

VENOM: Nah, man, he just wants to hear the S. word.

KKK: Nah, he wants us to feel the S word. He wants us to restore his faith in 'umanity. Regret the buzz we got from smashing his bitch's face. Repent the high we got from destroying his dream. He wants to believe again that black folks ain't all bad. He wants to feel okay for still loving us despite everything – for still wanting to be us. He don't want to face the fact he ain't a real nigga and he's just a tourist. He don't want to meet the people who live here and deal with reality. He wants to live in his dream world and for it all to all make sense. Innit, Wiggaboy?

EGGY: Is that it, white boy? Is that the miracle you're here for?

JJ: I just wanted a look at you. (*Pause.*) …Thanks.

He gets up and without a look back – leaves.

EGGY: That's it, batty bwoy! Gwan wit' your nasty-raas self! (*Turns back to the others…*) Well, that was fun…

ILLMANICS: …Next!

ORLANDO & JJ's flat

ORLANDO comes scampering in, giggling – We hear SAM offstage.

SAM: (*Offstage.*) Ten! Nine! Eight! Seven!

Breathless, ORLANDO looks around frantically. There is only a chair.

SAM enters – eyes still closed and feeling his way…

Six! Five-Four-Three…

ORLANDO squeals and wriggles under the woefully inadequate chair.

Two!

ORLANDO: (*To himself.*) …shhhhh! Shh shh shhhhh!

SAM: One.

SAM opens his eyes… He looks around – ORLANDO squirms and stifles a giggle…

Hmmmm! Why is it so dark in here..? I must get my eyes seen to… I can barely see a thing!

SAM sits on the chair, ORLANDO is beside himself with barely repressed glee.

Now, where is that wily little Orlando? I tell you, he's just too clever for me – I just give up – I'm off home to finish waxing, these eyebrows are galloping out of control…

ORLANDO crawls out excitedly.

ORLANDO: Here I am!

SAM: Where?

ORLANDO: Here!

SAM: (*Turning in circles.*) Who's that? Who's talking?

ORLANDO: (*Racing round him.*) Me, me! I'm here! Here I am!

SAM: (*Hugging ORLANDO.*) Oh my God! There you are, you master of disguise!

He sees a puddle under the chair. Reaching round he feels ORLANDO's bottom and finds a wet patch.

Oops – a touch damp in the rump – It's wipin' time! (*Pats ORLANDO's butt.*) Panties off, Principissa –

ORLANDO starts to take off his trousers –

ORLANDO: Awww, flip! Have I sat in something again?

SAM: No, love – you've pissed yourself. Don't sit on the floor, you'll make another puddle. Chop chop, we don't want nappy rash…

ORLANDO: (*Feet struggling with trousers.*) They won't come off! My shoes are too big!

SAM: Okay, sit down then…it's fine.

ORLANDO sits, SAM takes ORLANDO's trousers off over the shoes.

Here we go, Houdini – here's how we take our trousers off whilst keeping our shoes on – A skill every man should master…

ORLANDO: You're so clever – you can do everything. Are you going to stay here and live with us forever and ever?

SAM: Young man, you've known me a month.

ORLANDO: I love you, Sammy.

SAM: Sam. You like me. You love JJ.

ORLANDO: Yes. But when I tell JJ he looks sad.

SAM: That's men for you – can't handle commitment. Just keep telling him anyway 'til he smiles. You have to wear 'em down.

ORLANDO leans forward and gives SAM a deep lingering kiss.

SAM rolls up ORLANDO's now-removed trousers.

Mmm. You've been drinking milk again. You know it give you the runs.

ORLANDO starts to take off his pants.

Er, No! Keep the underwear on for a moment, 'til I fetch some clean ones, alright?

SAM hurries out…

And save the kisses for JJ okay, darling? They're all for JJ.

ORLANDO: Excuse me.

There is a tone in ORLANDO's voice that stops SAM.

Sam, it it?

SAM: Yes, Orlando?

ORLANDO is suddenly somehow his own age again.

87

ORLANDO: What's wrong with me?

SAM: You've had an accident, love, and you've been sick.

ORLANDO: It's something in my brain, isn't it?

SAM: You've got brain damage. But here you are
    – miraculously cured!

ORLANDO: But it won't last, will it?

SAM: You come and go.

ORLANDO: Yes, I think I remember, almost. You're
    pretty…are you seeing JJ? No. You're the home help.
    Sorry… (*Looking round.*) It's summer now, isn't it?

    I love summer, don't I? They're never long enough in
    London. When you see JJ will you tell him I miss him?
    Just in case I forget?

SAM: I will – but try and remember, eh?

ORLANDO: Ooh… I stink…

SAM: I'll fetch your clean knickers.

    SAM exits.

ORLANDO: My bum's sore…

    *ORLANDO, a child again, sprawls out on the ground in
    frustration…*

    Sameee! My bum's sore!

    SOUND: Door opening.

    ORLANDO leaps up.

    JJ!

JJ enters. ORLANDO descends and peppers him with kisses.

JJ: Orly? Where's your trousers to?

ORLANDO: Hey JJ. What do you say? Do you want to play the gay boy way? Orly and JJ sittin' in a tree – K-i-s-s-i-n-g...

JJ: Where's Sam? Have you scared him off?

Sam!

Orly, babe...

Sam!

I got something for you...

He produces a sparkler and lighter.

Ohhh...!

JJ hands it the glittering & fizzing firework to ORLANDO.

ORLANDO: Ohhhhhhhhlılıhhhhhhh! Jay Jaaayyyyy!

JJ: Orly – you're soaked! Sam!

SAM enters...

SAM: Present, Sir!

JJ: Orly's soaked.

SAM: I'm running a bath. Orly, come!

JJ: I'll do it.

SOUND: Doorbell.

Pause.

SAM: Seeing as I don't live here, I'm guessing that's for you.

JJ: Take Orly to the bathroom, will you, please.

SAM leads JJ off to the bathroom.

SAM: Come on, skunky bum…

JJ: And lock the door, yeah?

JJ approaches the front door.

Who the fuck's that?

DANIEL: Mr Johannson? I'm Daniel Pearl. I represented the defence at the recent trial.

JJ: 'Daniel Pearl'?

DANIEL: I'm sorry to have bothered you at home.

JJ opens the door.

JJ: What do you want?

DANIEL: Justice. I know you believe that if your partner's attackers had been jailed for life – justice would have been served – It would not. As repellent and depressing as they are – those ignorant bullies are not what has caused you this unspeakable suffering. They are merely the carriers of a disease that struck your lover down. I used to believe this disease was society. Struggling to make sense of this senselessness, to fathom this brutality – Until yesterday, while searching for the BBC World Service on my car radio – recently replaced after my sixth break-in – I came across an extraordinary sound – bass, drums, chanting voices – hypnotically rhythmic. I never dance, but here I was nodding to the beat – So seductive, so stirring, so bloody sexy. And then an extraordinary voice two parts earth and one part sweet molasses chanting a familiar phrase. One I've heard in interview rooms and young offenders units, countless irritating times. And now here it was, pumping through my body, over and over – hijacking the very pattern of my corruptible heartbeat – until I found myself chanting too. 'Chi-chi man, Chi-chi man – Chi-chi man fe dead'. I've googled Chi-chi on the net – Do you know what it means? Termite. Cockroach…

DANIEL / JJ: …Vermin.

DANIEL: And I was singing along. With words I barely understood. And then I looked to my right and I saw that the kids in the next car – shaven heads, tracksuits, diamond earrings, you know the type – were singing along with me. Tuned into the same station and singing the same words. Our brains were being colonised – infected. I think you should take out a civil case against the composers, producers and performers responsible for these records. They are the disease. We can be the cure. (*Pause.*) And that, perhaps, might be something like justice.

ORLANDO enters in a towelling robe, wet head and wet feet…

ORLANDO: JJ. JJ!

JJ: Stay in the bathroom, babe, I'll be there in a minute…

ORLANDO: Look at my footsteps! I'm Robinson Crusoe!

JJ: Man Friday, Orly.

SAM: More of a wet weekend, I'd say… Come on, soggy, let's sort out your toes before you get trenchfoot and fuck up my CV. (*Seeing DANIEL.*) Oh. Hello.

DANIEL: Hello Sam.

ORLANDO: Hello!

KEVAN arrives.

KEVAN: Hey you! How'd it go? (*Seeing DANIEL.*) Oh, hello. Who are you?

SAM: This is Daniel.

ORLANDO: Hello, Daniel!

DANIEL: Hello Orlando.

KEVAN: Daniel?

JJ: He was the defence lawyer in…

KEVAN: I know who he is. What's he doing here?

DANIEL: I wanted to have a quick word.

KEVAN: How about cunt? That's a quick word.

JJ: Kevan.

KEVAN: Come to gloat have you? Fucking cunt!

JJ: Kevan. (*To DANIEL.*) Come in a minute, yeah?

DANIEL: Thanks.

DANIEL & KEVAN step into the flat.

JJ: Sam, could you get Orly dressed, please?

SAM: Come on little mermaid. Let's get you fit for dry land.

SAM leads ORLANDO off.

JJ: So you think it's that simple? The Music.

DANIEL: Music is influential. That's why there are National Anthems. And hymns and football chants.

JJ: So, if there were no football chants there'd be no hooligans?

DANIEL: Music can be a rallying cry.

JJ: Music can be a lot of things.

DANIEL: What is it to you?

JJ: It's everything. It never made me hurt anyone. Before I found Orly, Music was the only thing that could help me.

DANIEL: Did it help you be queer?

JJ: This was before I knew I was queer.

DANIEL: And when you finally did know did the Music help then? Or hinder?

KEVAN: What the fuck are you two talking about?

DANIEL: Music. What does it mean to you?

KEVAN: To me? Depends on the music.

DANIEL opens his backpack and pulls out an iPod and pair of portable speakers. He starts to hook them up...

DANIEL: ... May I?

JJ shrugs... DANIEL deftly completes the connection and presses play – we hear an infectious ragga tune...

What does this music mean to you? First thoughts and words that come in your head...

KEVAN: Black music. Ragga. Dancehall. Dance music. Sexy.

SOUND: iPod.

VOCAL: Boom! Go a gat in a batty-bwoy brain!

DANIEL presses pause.

DANIEL: Did you get that?

KEVAN: Boom something?

DANIEL reads from the CD cover…

DANIEL: Conveniently it's the title… 'Boom! Go a Gat In a Batty-Boy Brain.' JJ? 'Gat'?

JJ: Gun.

DANIEL: 'Batty-boy…'?

KEVAN: I know what batty-boys are.

DANIEL: … And I think the word 'brain' is universal – 'Boom go a gat in a batty-boy's brain – Bang goes a gun in a queer-boy's brain'.

SAM enters, unnoticed, as DANIEL releases pause.

VOCAL: Gwan, pull a trigga inna Nigga brudda name.

DANIEL: 'Go on, pull a trigger in the name of black men…'

VOCAL: Sen' a chi-chi man a hell wit a…

JJ snaps it off.

DANIEL: 'Send a chi-chi man to hell with a spike in the eye.'

KEVAN: Jesus Christ, JJ. That's fucked up.

JJ: It's just music.

KEVAN: Is that what they're all saying?

DANIEL: When I was sixteen the first Lenny Kravitz album was my bible. It was more than music.

JJ: And if he told you to go out and shoot people, would you have done it? No Kevan, that's not what they're all saying.

KEVAN: Just some of them? That's fucking insane, JJ.

JJ: The world's insane, Kevan – there are nutcases everywhere – Some of 'em make records – Some of 'em make brilliant records – Freedom of speech can be fucked up but that's democracy. (*To DANIEL.*) You haven't answered my question.

DANIEL: If Lenny Kravitz had told me to go out and shoot people, would I have done it?... No.

JJ: And why not?

SAM: 'Cause he's a nice well-educated white boy. And they're a bunch of impressionable jungle-bunnies who don't know better.

DANIEL: You know that's not what I mean.

SAM: And do you know what you mean?

DANIEL: Have you listened to this music?

SAM: I've heard it.

DANIEL: And you find it acceptable?

SAM: I find it...painful.

DANIEL: So, are we going to just let them hurt us?

SAM: Some people find the sight of two men kissing painful – are they right to make it illegal?

DANIEL: No, they find it offensive.

SAM: No, they find it painful.

DANIEL: Those are their issues – These are our lives. Are you suggesting challenging black people on homophobia is racism?

SAM: Are you planning to picket any white artists?

DANIEL: Like?

SAM: Like Eminem? Multi-platinum selling homophobic Eminem? 'Sexy' white-trash Eminem who doesn't do interviews with gay magazines who write about him anyway Eminem?

DANIEL: Eminem doesn't advocate murder.

SAM: Isn't there a line in there about raping a lesbian? Oh, wait – I forgot – that was a joke. He's funny.

DANIEL: Okay…maybe we should consider suing Eminem.

SAM: Here's the thing, Daniel. Black people expect to be under attack. If you go after the handful of black people who are making any money, all we'll see is another white man trying to take our power. It won't work.

DANIEL: 'We'?

SAM: We.

DANIEL: Sam. You're gay.

SAM: And black. Or didn't you notice?

DANIEL: I noticed. You're black. And the enemy is every colour under sun. Today they happen to be black, tomorrow they'll be something else.

SAM: 'The enemy'.

DANIEL: Not because they're black – because they're trying to hurt us. If I was here today talking about rock music would you join us?

SAM: I don't know.

DANIEL: Well, join us. Work with us. Help us.

SAM: 'Us'?

DANIEL looks round at JJ and KEVAN.

DANIEL: Me. Join me.

KEVAN: Us.

SAM: I won't be the golliwog on the dust-cart.

DANIEL: ⎱ ⎰ Sorry?

KEVAN: ⎰ ⎱ Do what?

SAM: I won't be the mascot. Proof that you're good non-racist white folks.

DANIEL: Okay.

SAM: I'll go educational but not oppositional.

DANIEL: Okay. Um. What does that mean?

SAM: Each one, teach one. Outreach.

DANIEL: Oh. Okay.

KEVAN: Now, let's not overdo it, okay? Not everyone needs a hug, you know – some people need a slap, and some of them are black.

SAM: And some of them are not.

KEVAN: Don't you ever just want to open a can of kick-ass?

SAM: You mean now?

DANIEL: Okay, you two…

KEVAN: What happened to 'By Any Means Neccessary'?

DANIEL: Gentlemen, please, whatever the colour, the enemy is not in this room. Perhaps we could agree to deal with these issues on a case-by-case basis?

DANIEL & KEVAN shrug.

SAM: OK.

KEVAN: Cool.

DANIEL: JJ?

ALL look at JJ.

Prison hallway

VENOM is mopping the floor… WHITE FANG passes slowly holding a tray of food, head bowed, his face badly bruised.

VENOM: (*Whispering, not looking up.*) Yo! Yo, Blood!

VENOM dares to move closer.

Yo, Fang me brudda. Whassappening? Why ain't you speak with me, blood? Yo!

WHITE FANG: Come away from me, man.

VENOM: Is wha' you say?

WHITE FANG: Come away from me – we can't speak, man. They're watching.

VENOM: Fuck them, man, they can't hear.

WHITE FANG: Not the screws, man.

VENOM: You mean them cell-mates you got?

WHITE FANG: Yeah man. They got a problem with coons, man, innit? They ain't feeling 'em for real.

VENOM: Fang man… What the fuck you just call me? What's that on your face, bruv?

VENOM makes a move towards WHITE FANG – who drops the tray with a metallic crash to reveal that he is carrying a large chisel… VENOM stares at it.

Man, what the fuck you doing? We're spars, man – we're brothas!

WHITE FANG: (*Loud.*) I know you, nigger? I fucking know you? (*Whispers.*) Walk away, blood…

VENOM: Fang, blood…

WHITE FANG: I'm begging you bruv… Walk.

VENOM: You know I can't step with every muthafucka watching, man…

WHITE FANG: Then you know I gotta fuck you up.

VENOM: We ain't gotta play this game, blood, we can stand together, shake hands and stay strong. We can represent. (*Steps forward.*) …blood…

WHITE FANG: Nigger!

WHITE FANG punches VENOM clean in the face. VENOM goes down. WHITE FANG leaps into a straddle position, chisel held in both hands above his head…panting, but never striking, panting panting…

VENOM grabs the tray and hits WHITE FANG in the side of the head, and in a second, their positions are reversed.

VENOM straddling WHITE FANG with the chisel held aloft.

Do it! Please man, for me, man!

VENOM: For you?

WHITE FANG: They've seen me fail, man. They'll fucking crucify me! Just the eye. In the eye, yeah? Please man, I'm fucking begging you, man! Release me, man!

VENOM: Julian, man…

WHITE FANG punches VENOM in the face.

WHITE FANG: White Fang, you fucking coon! WHITE Fang! (*Punching.*) You fucking ignorant fucking jungle bunny!

VENOM (*Agonised.*) Fuck, man…!

WHITE FANG: Fucking monkey! Fucking baboon! Fucking gorilla monkey coon!

VENOM stabs down, the knife hovers above WHITE FANG's eye.

(*Sounds like a monkey.*) Oo oo oo oo oo oo oo oo oo…

VENOM stabs down.

Blackout.

Exercise studio

Five punch-bags suspended from above.

DANIEL, SAM, KEVAN & ORLANDO & JJ dressed to exercise. ORLANDO wearing headphones and dancing..

DANIEL: Welcome to the first gathering of Lashback – a self defence group for lesbian, gay, transgender, bisexual and questioning queers of all persuasions. Obviously right now the only representatives are, well…

SAM: … Gay.

DANIEL: …but with our imminent non-confrontational initiative against the death-mongerers of ragga as our first major public platform I believe that this David can grow to become a Goliath that can defend us and our sisters and brothers from the omnipresent threat of unprovoked attack. Kicking butt in the name of Love.

OTHERS: Kicking butt in the name of Love!

SAM: (*To JJ.*) JJ sister, where d'you want us?

JJ: Well, firstly, we need to assess everyone's basic fighting ability. Everyone by their punch-bags, yeah? Orly, babe… (*Removing ORLANDO's headphones.*) You wanna play?

ORLANDO: Okay!

DANIEL, SAM & KEVAN stand by their punchbags.

JJ: Okay! The punch-bag is the enemy – you have to defend yourself – do what you can – go!

JJ starts punching – Nobody else moves.

You're facing a drunk hard-faced bastard who's about to punch your face in with a knuckle-dustered fist – what do you do?

ORLANDO opens his arms and hugs his punch-bag…

SAM: Aw bless! Some people never learn.

JJ: Sam – what would you do?

SAM: Me? Well, there's a trick I learned from my grandmother – who be know as the Battling Bitch from Brixton… (*Doing as he speaks.*) They're facing you down, you maintain eye contact, but gradually lower your centre of gravity as if curtsying in supplication and subordination, until you can slip off your shoe – (*Slipping off shoe.*) – and batter! The fucker! (*Attacking punch-bag with shoe.*) Round! The face! (*Running off.*) And run! Non-confrontationally of course…

KEVAN: With only one shoe?

SAM: Not very graceful when you're in heels – but hey – survival is the ultimate glamour.

JJ: Okayyyy, now – ball the fist up – do not tuck the thumb inside – you don't want to break it – aim to connect with this part of the fist here – stand far back enough for the arm to be almost extended on impact – pull back… and punch!

ALL – except ORLANDO – punch – with a satisfying whack.

KEVAN / SAM / DANIEL (*pleasantly surprised.*) Oh! Mmm! (etc)

JJ: Feels good, don't it?

KEVAN / SAM / DANIEL: Mmm!

JJ: Now just picture whoever releases your anger, yeah?

He leads them in a rhythmic punching.

– a mugger – (*Punch.*) – a homophobe – (*Punch.*) – abusive ex –

Big punch.

– school bully – (*Punch.*) – teacher…

KEVAN: (*Punching hard.*) Bastard!

JJ: Kevan?

KEVAN: (*Punching hard.*) Bastard! Bastard! Bastard!
(*Frenzied.*) Fucking fucking bastard bastard!

JJ: (*Stopping him.*) Kevan!

KEVAN pants…

Well done – take a breath – you okay?

KEVAN: I'm great – this cunt is dead though! (*Battering
punchbag.*) Dead! Fucking cunt! Nasty! Dirty!
Homophobic! Cunt!

DANIEL: I applaud your ability to access your anger,
Kevan – but the c-word is offensive to many lesbians
and gay men.

KEVAN: Cunt! Fucker! Cunt! Cunt! (*Crying.*) Cunt! Cunt!
Cunt! Cunt!

*ORLANDO puts his arms round KEVAN who breaks
down, weeping… ORLANDO rocks him in his arms…*

Bastard…

Silence – except for KEVAN's weeping… then…

SAM: Nice cup of tea anyone?

DANIEL (*Snatching up his wallet.*) Good – on me?

SAM: On you sounds great!

*SAM and DANIEL exit. JJ gently prises KEVAN &
ORLANDO apart, handing KEVAN a towel…*

KEVAN: God, I'm turning into such a total cry-baby.

JJ slips ORLANDO's headphones back over his ears. ORLANDO still holding onto his hands, dances round him...

JJ: What's going on, Kevan?

KEVAN: What's going on? You're going to stand there with Orly right beside you and ask me what's going on? We're being massacred! (*Breathing.*) ...Oh shit. I'm sorry. It's just knowing they get released so soon. And there's you so...fucking...staunch – I don't know if I'm pissed off with you or in awe. Maybe I just need a boyfriend.

JJ: Well, I can recommend that.

KEVAN: Sorry. I suppose we're both a bit out of practice. Maybe we should help each other out.

JJ: Oh?

KEVAN: Maybe go for a drink before the demonstration on Friday?

JJ looks blank.

Friday? We're picketing that gig by that reggae dude – Lego Man?

JJ: Lion Man.

KEVAN: Yeah, him. We could go to that bar in New Cross just before, check out the babes and have a flirt – what do you reckon?

JJ: Kevan, I know the picket is needed – Statements have to be made – life has to be lived – and cute boys need to be loved. But I don't know if I can do anything except love Orly and the music.

KEVAN: How can you still love that music, after all it's done?

JJ: It's not the music.

KEVAN: If it's not the music, then what is it?

JJ: These are the questions that chew me up, 'til it feels like there's nothing left over.

KEVAN: Nothing? Not even a little bit? I'm a student, I'm used to feasting on crumbs. We're both here, mate. Why do we have to be alone?

JJ: I don't know. Maybe we don't.

KEVAN: So, it's a date? …ette?

JJ: It's a datette.

KEVAN: What is that Orly's listening to?

JJ: Just some random tracks I downloaded for him…

KEVAN goes over to ORLANDO lifts a headphone for a quick listen. ORLANDO gives JJ a kiss. JJ replaces the headphone.

KEVAN: Lion Man?

JJ: Don't tell Daniel. (*Grins apologetically.*) Orly loves it.

Prison visiting room

KARISMA waits… KKK enters. They look at one another.

KKK: You came, then.

KARISMA: I wonder which of us is more surprised.

KKK: You remember me? Who I am?

KARISMA: Your name's KKK and you like a Twix?

KKK: Your name is Karisma and you don't take no shit.

KARISMA: (*Looking round.*) Never been in a prison before.

KKK: You're lucky.

KARISMA: How long you in here?

KKK: Too long.

KARISMA: What you here for?

KKK: We don't ask them questions in here.

KARISMA: Okay… What am I here for?

KKK shrugs. KARISMA produces a letter.

'Dear Miss Karisma, I'm sorry, but I do not know your full name so please forgive my overfamiliarity. I also hope you can forgive my writing to you at your place of work, but I wanted to inform you that I am now a resident of Her Majesty's Prison and to ask if you could find the time and the generosity somewhere in your heart to come and visit me. You are probably wondering why – If you visit I will explain. Regards, Dijon Socrates Lawrence the third aka KKK.'

She folds the letter and waits.

KKK: I tried hating you – dismissing you. Demonising you. But you'd taken over a room in my brain and you were holding a part of me hostage. So I gave in and writ you. I never thought in a million years you'd actually come.

KARISMA: So why'd you write, then?

KKK: In a place like this fantasy's what gets you through it.

KARISMA: So you're not gonna ask me to be a drug mule? Bake you a cake with a file in it?… Show you my tits while you wank furtively? Well, I'm disappointed. I was looking forward to being outraged. Is it that shameful?

KKK: Shameful?

KARISMA: What you've done? Is that why you can't tell me? Are you ashamed?

KKK: Ain't I tell you? We don't talk about them things in here.

KARISMA: I ain't in there.

KKK: No, I am. And you're out there – judging me. (*Turns away.*) Well, thanks for coming, yeah? Fucking bitch!

KARISMA: (*Pause.*) You're welcome.

She gets up, turns and starts to leave…

KKK: Gwan, skank, fucking run! Run like everybody else runs. Run from the fucking devil – Gwan! Run from your own shame!

KARISMA stops.

Yeah, woman. Your shame. The shame you feel when you look at me. Another black man in jail. Another black man bringing down the race. Another black man with no shame. (*Pause.*) I ain't got no shame. I don't know why. Weren't I born with none? Was it kicked out of me? Did I lose it on the way? Or did you get my share? Are you walking out the door with my only hope for redemption? Are you gonna forget me? Am I done? Am I over? The lost cause? Is that what I am? Is that me?

KARISMA looks at KKK – then sits down.

KARISMA: Don't tell me – you're innocent.

KKK: Who's innocent in this world? You? The truth is,
sista, I'm a liar. I tell lies. I lie to my mother 'bout
where the bling comes from. I lie to my babymother
'bout where I been. Even them rare days when there's
nothing to hide, I lie just to keep in practice. I am a
fucking lie. P'raps the reason I writ you and no-one else
is to see if I could deal with another living person and
not bother with lies. Let's face it, your expectations so
low of me you can't be disappointed. (*Pause.*)

I was in a fight.

KARISMA: A fight?

KKK: An attack. I attacked someone. Hurt 'em bad. Brain
damage.

KARISMA: Why?

KKK: He was gay. He was white. He was there. I disgust
you. You hate me, innit?

KARISMA: I don't know. Did you hate him?

KKK: I didn't know him. Actually… Yes! Man and man
together – it just – it ain't right. That's in the Bible.

KARISMA: Know the Bible well, do you?

KKK: I know that part.

KARISMA: You a Christian, then?

KKK: 'S how I was raised.

KARISMA: Finally, something in common. I was a big
fan of Jesus growing up. He said such cool things – 'If
thine eye offend thee, pluck it out.' 'Judge not lest ye
be judged.'… Not a word about homosexuality, funnily

enough as I recall – 'cept maybe 'Blessed are they that are persecuted for righteousness' sake'?

KKK: Gays ain't persecuted – they're promoted. They're all over the TV and that. They got sitcoms! Where's our sitcoms? They practically got ads saying, 'Be gay! Be funny! Give straight men make-overs like we can't dress ourselves!' What if everyone was gay? The human race would die out innit? It's our purpose to breed. Our imperative.

KARISMA: How many kids you got?

KKK: Four.

KARISMA: Don't think there's much chance of the human race dying out with you around, mate.

KKK: Look, you ain't gonna convince me it's cool and dandy for one man to kiss on another man like it's normal, 'cause you know it ain't.

KARISMA: I think it's beautiful.

KKK: It ain't natural.

KARISMA: What's natural? This plastic chair we're sitting on? The food we eat? Shaving? Tampons? Cars? Laser surgery? I've seen you in your tracksuit – not a natural fibre in sight.

KKK: It all comes from nature in the beginning though, don't it? Plastic, Nylon – it all has to come from somewhere before it's refined, yeah? So it's all natural yeah? (*Realising what he's said, kissing his teeth.*) Think you're well cleverer 'n me, innit? This chi-chi man weren't natural. Him act like a gyal.

KARISMA: And you don't like girls?

KKK: Now you're just talking stupid. You know what I'm saying… Man is man, and woman is woman. That's how the system works… You want your man to be a man don't you?

KARISMA: I want everyone to be themselves.

KKK: Well, I'm a man who don't like queers – that's me. What? You want me to apologise? You know how hard it is to be me? To be a man in this world? In this life? A black man? You don't know. You can't know. Black woman's pain don't compare, you hear.

KARISMA: I'm not qualified to compare.

KKK: Well, I am.

KARISMA: Oh really.

KKK: Yeah really. Nuff spare time inna dis place, yunno. I been reading – researching. Black women's four times more employed, five times more likely to do well in school. Nine times less likely to end up in jail.

KARISMA: And black woman should apologise for black man's failure in the system?

KKK: She should be aware of how the system is failing her man. She should get it. She should support her soldier.

KARISMA: 'Soldier'?

KKK: This is a war, woman! And you want me to indulge some white boy's privilege to be soft? He was there – up in our club – up in our music all up in our face – what did he expect? A kiss and a cuddle? Or what he got?

KARISMA: So, that's what you've brought me here to tell me? That you've got no soft side?

KKK: You what?

She eyes KKK's painted nail – he snatches it out of view.

KARISMA: No gentle side, no graceful side – No elegance yearning in you?

KKK: What the fuck you talking 'bout?

KARISMA: Just a wall of man with no way in and no keyhole of tenderness anywhere?

KKK: What you trying here, gyal? You trying to mess with a brotha's mind?

KARISMA: I don't know. Is that why I'm here?

SOUND: Buzzer.

KKK: Shit.

KARISMA: Time's up.

KKK: Already. Muthafuckas don't give you nuttin'. You ain't coming again?

KARISMA: You inviting me?

KKK: I never had a chat like this before. Prob'ly you went college, yeah? Conversation's normal to you.

KARISMA: Trust me – this is all brand new.

KKK: (*Unsure.*) So…?

KARISMA: So?

KKK: So next month? If I try and come up with a little sump'in to show you? Like, on the feminine side?

KARISMA: How could a girl resist?

KKK: I'll work on it.

Interview room

KKK sits in silence, watching...

SOUND: Door opening.

WHITE FANG enters, his face battered.

KKK: Yo.

WHITE FANG: 'sup.

WHITE FANG sits.

SOUND: Door opening.

EGGY & VENOM enter – WHITE FANG turns away as KKK, EGGY & VENOM exchange handshakes.

EGGY: Bruv...

VENOM: Bruv...

KKK: Whaddup...

SOUND: Door opening.

Enter JJ.

JJ: Was it the music?

Silence.

EGGY: You had me at hello.

The ILLMANICS smile to themselves – but make no eye contact.

JJ: Was it the music that made you do it? Did you chant lyrics while you beat his brains out? Was it church? Did the preacher inspire you to despise people who fall in love without your permission? Did you learn it in school? In the playground? At home? Where does it all come from? The laws in Jamaica and Africa? Brainwashing you? Where does the rage begin? Or did someone come out of nowhere to crush your life underfoot when you weren't looking? Should I be in the hate already? See, I envy you. I want to feel nothing just like you do. I wanna laugh about you being in here just like you do. I wanna not give a fuck about all this. I want to hate.

Silence. JJ gets to his feet, goes to the door.

SOUND: Door opening.

SAM comes in. JJ walks back to the centre of the room.

JJ: This is Sam.

SAM holds open the door.

SAM: Come on, trouble…

ORLANDO runs in, playing aeroplanes.

ORLANDO: Eeeeeeeeeoooooooooow! Eeeeeeooooowww!

JJ: This is Orly.

ORLANDO: Eeeeeeeooooooooovoowwwww! I'm an airplane!

JJ: You're an excellent airplane, Orly – but I just want you to meet some people, okay?

ORLANDO: Okay.

JJ: You know how you like meeting people, Orly. You like making new friends, yeah?

ORLANDO: (*Smiling bashfully.*) Yeah.

JJ: Well, this is Marquis…

ORLANDO: Hi!

JJ: That's Duran..

ORLANDO: Hi!

JJ: Dijon Socrates the third…

ORLANDO: Hi!

JJ: And Julian.

ORLANDO: Hello! (*Looking round.*) Everyone's so sad!

> *ORLANDO heads towards VENOM, arms open. VENOM darts away.*

VENOM: DON'T FUCKING TOUCH ME, YOU FUCKING QUEER!

EGGY: Oy! Leave my boy, yeah?

> *JJ steps in front of EGGY, gently pulls ORLANDO to him.*

JJ: …Orly.

ORLANDO: I'm sorry, JJ. I just wanted to give him a cuddle.

JJ: I know, baby – it's cool. Sam…

SAM (*Taking custody of ORLANDO.*) Come away from the bad men, lovely.

EGGY: So this is your secret weapon is it? The spastic and his mammy?

SAM: Is who you a' call Mammy, bwoy?

EGGY: Who the fuck are you calling 'bwoy', Mammy?

> *They kiss their teeth.*

JJ: I just wanted you to meet Orly.

EGGY: Bullshit. You just wanted to fuck us up and you brought along Aunt Jemima here to prove that you ain't a racist! Well, I got news for you, white boy – that ain't black – that's a fucking coconut!

SAM: Sing us another song while you're on the chain-gang. I'm a coconut because I'm gay?

EGGY: Because you're a traitor to your race. I bet your father's well proud of you, innit?

SAM: And I bet your mamma's well proud of you, Prisoner eight-six-six-six one-zero – innit?

They kiss their teeth.

I told you this was a waste of time, JJ. What the hell are we doing here?

EGGY: Yeah, What are you doing here? Ain't you had enough yet? Coming here – arxing questions – Like answers exist. What the fuck it you really want to know? Why did this happen? To you – the Niggalover? Why do Niggas hate Niggalovers? Why do Niggas hate queers? Why do Niggas hate everyone – even other Niggas? Cause that's what Niggas do. Niggas hate.

JJ: Not all, man.

EGGY: All.

JJ: Not all black people are Niggas.

EGGY: See, white boy, that's what you ain't been getting. Everyone's a nigga. Every last one of us. Ain't you? Why did you wanna be a MC – all the way out there in cow country? Because you wanted to be a Nigga? Or because you knew you were a one?

Silence.

What was it you related to? The passion? The rage for how fucked up and uneven and unfair this world is? The rage for how it makes you feel? You come here talking 'bout how you wanna feel the hate. Bullshit. You already feel it. We all feel it. We're all Niggas and we all hate queers. Including you.

JJ: Me?

EGGY: Yeah – you.

SAM: Yeah… You.

EGGY: Aren't you here with all us? Under the same laws – and the same religions?

SAM: You watch your hands in conversation and wonder how gay you look – You build up an armour of muscles, like a billboard, that advertises your masculinity. And still you wonder what earthly use you are if you don't procreate – you wonder what it is that made you queer – was you born like it or did your mother rock you wrong in the cradle – have you got a woman's brain in a man's body? What the fuck are you? Why the fuck are you? You march and you chant and laugh in the face of those who spit and shit on you and tell yourself you can be gay and proud and still be a man –

EGGY: – That you can be black in this world and still be a man –

SAM: – but there's the doubt –

EGGY: – and there's the hate –

SAM: – and there's your nigga.

EGGY: Here's your nigga. Different muscles…

EGGY / SAM: …same nigga.

EGGY: Trying to be a man in a world that says you can't. Trying to be here in a world that says you ain't.

SAM: And the best you manage is to be a cartoon.

EGGY: Yeah. It's the music. And the preacher and the playground and the parents – and yeah, them laws back home that was put in place back in the day by the British Empire – The same laws that was in place inna dis 'ere country not so long ago. It's alla dat – and more. There ain't one reason why Niggas hate queers – there's every reason.

SAM: 'Cause we're all queers…

EGGY: …and we're all Niggas. Struggling to be men. Unable to handle you and your boy there fucking. Forget all this men loving men bullshit – it's the fucking that's the mind fuck. Men getting fucked – too close to the situation a nigga's living – you feel me, nigga?

JJ: (*Pause.*) Yeah. I feel you, nigga. (*Pause.*) Thank you.

JJ raises his fist. EGGY looks at it.

EGGY: For what? Helping you find your hate? It was always there, man.

JJ: For helping me find my truth.

EGGY looks around at the ILLMANICS, WHITE FANG is staring at the wall, disassociated. VENOM is looking at the floor. KKK is watching, still as a cat. EGGY is alone.

EGGY: And what's that, then?

JJ: That hate is weakness. And lovers can't afford to be weak.

EGGY: Now, I know you ain't calling us weak, man…

JJ: 'These are the words of my master, keep on telling me, no weak hearts shall prosper. And whosoever diggeth a pit, Shall…'

VENOM: 'Fall in it… Shall bury in it.'

EGGY: So, you know your Marley.

JJ: He's my prophet, man. 'I don't fear their humiliation – Just to prove my determination –'

JJ / VENOM: 'I don't yield to temptation –'

JJ / VENOM / EGGY: 'I haven't learned my lesson in revelation.'

EGGY: 'The road of life is rocky – and you may stumble too – and while you point your finger – someone else is judging you.'

JJ: 'Would you let the system make you kill your brother man?

JJ / VENOM: 'No dread no…'

JJ: 'Well the biggest man you ever did see was…'

They look at ORLANDO…

VENOM: 'A baby…' 'Open your eyes and look within – are you satisfied with the life you're living?'

'Most people think Great God will come from the sky – Take everything and make everyone feel high – but if you know what life is worth then you will look for yours on Earth…' (*Deep painful breath.*) We goin' a Hell, innit, man?

EGGY: Hush man.

VENOM: We're already gone, innit? We're already there. 'Let them all pass their dirty remarks – there's only one thing I'd really like to arx – Is there a place for the hopeless sinner – who has hurt mankind just to save his own.' Our grandmother she come to see us in here just one time. I had to beg her never again. To see her cry like that – so heartbroke. (*In torment.*) I wanted to die man, I wanted to fucking die!

Distressed, EGGY starts towards VENOM, but cannot hold him.

EGGY: Cuz, cuz, cuz… Hush…

VENOM: Oh fuck, man…we're there, man, burning for sure. For sure…lost, lost, our souls is lost…

ORLANDO walks up and puts his arms around an unresisting VENOM and rocks him.

How do we reach forgiveness from here, man? Which way redemption?

JJ: Wish I knew man. For real. Wish I could find forgiveness myself. But I can't hate you and I can't forgive you. All there is -- is this.

EGGY: Hit me, man.

JJ looks at EGGY.

Hard as you like. We gotta do something innit? If we want to move on. Hit me.

JJ: You wanna move on?

EGGY: Look at us, man. Look where we are. We got to move on – or die or something. Yeah. I wanna move on. I wanna feel – whassit – remorse. I wanna be sorry. And you want vengeance, don't you? So just hit me, yeah? For all of us.

JJ: I ain't gonna hit you, man. But thanks for asking, yeah?

EGGY: Well, listen if you ever change your mind – you know where I am. Or if you wanna talk about anything, music or Marley or whatever, that's cool. Cool?

EGGY raises his fist.

JJ: Cool.

JJ & EGGY touch knuckles – fist to fist.

Visiting room

KARISMA enters to find KKK waiting.

KKK: You came back.

KARISMA: And you're still here.

KARISMA holds out a photograph. KKK looks at it.

Recognise these two people? Look closer. See it yet? My smile in his face, her eyes in mine?

KKK: I see it.

KARISMA: This was taken a week before he killed her. With his bare hands. She was getting texts from a man at work. He thought she was encouraging him. By the time I came home and found 'em he'd hung himself. Now tell me you're qualified to judge a black woman's pain. Don't worry, I'm not going to cry.

KKK: I'm sorry.

KARISMA: No, you're not. You don't know them.

KKK: I know you.

KARISMA: No, you don't.

KKK: I want to. And I want to be sorry. I'm ready to be sorry. See, I been thinking.

KARISMA: Thinking? What next? Feeling?

KKK: …about my feminine side. You wanna see it?

KARISMA: Oh go on, then, seeing as I'm here.

> *KKK yanks his pants down for a moment to expose a pair of silky knickers. KARISMA screams in delighted surprise.*

Why Miss Jones, you're beautiful. Where'd you get them? Agent Provocateur?

KKK: I bought 'em on eBay.

KARISMA: God bless the internet. That good am I? One visit and you're converted from lager lout to Lady-boy? No wonder I can't keep a man.

KKK: Don't worry about it – I had these before you.

KARISMA: Oh.

KKK: It's the thinking that's new…not the feeling. And all down to you. And I've been listening. Studying. You can cry now if you want. For your parents. I'll know what to do.

KARISMA: Which is?

KKK: Well, I can't hold you – not in here. But I'll want to. And I won't let you cry alone.

KARISMA: What happened to the soldier?

KKK: He's found something new to fight for.

KARISMA: Well. You really have been studying.

KKK: And learning. We are all niggers and we're all queers.

KARISMA: Now I'd wear that t-shirt.

KKK: (*Grins shyly…*) Gyal, you something else, you know that? Always got a line.

KARISMA: And you've got a pretty smile.

KKK produces a huge smile.

KKK: And you ain't got a man?

KARISMA: All the best men are queer.

They smile.

ORLANDO & JJ's flat

SOUND: Car horn outside.

JJ rushes in still dressing and deodorising,

JJ: Orly!

JJ opens the door, calls out…

One minute, yeah? Orly!

ORLANDO: I'm doing wee-wee!

VENOM comes out of the toilet.

VENOM: He's doing wee-wee.

JJ: He does that a lot.

EGGY enters with a backpack.

EGGY: We know.

JJ: His number twos can be a bit unpredictable as well.

EGGY / VENOM: We know!

JJ: So, you've got a couple of changes of clothes, in case, yeah?

EGGY (*Holding up backpack.*) Er…

JJ: And you've got both my mobile numbers, yeah?

EGGY: JJ man… Chill.

JJ: Yeah, I'm chilled, chilled, seen, seen. Only one icecream, yeah, or he'll eat 'til he's sick.

EGGY: It's cool, blood. I've got a kid myself, take her out every Thursday – I know the runnings.

ORLANDO: (*Offstage, approaching.*) Marky! Marky!

ORLANDO appears in the bathroom door.

Marky Mark!

VENOM: Marquis, Orly. Marquis. Did you flush?

ORLANDO: Come and check out this poo first (*Indicates 18 inches.*) – it's this long!

VENOM: Lead me to it, man, can't wait…

ORLANDO: Come on, before it sinks!

JJ: Orly… Orly…!

ORLANDO: What, JJ? Me and Marky are busy.

JJ: How about my goodbye kiss?

ORLANDO rolls his eyes, gives JJ a kiss then breezes off.

No hug?

ORLANDO: I haven't washed my hands.

JJ: I love you!

ORLANDO: I know.

JJ: And if he has one of his moments, if there's even a glimpse of the old Orly, you'll call me, yeah? I don't want to miss it.

EGGY: You're on speed-dial, now gwan!

JJ: Peace.

They brush fists.

EGGY: Peace. Go!

SOUND: Car horn.

JJ: Shit!

He runs out…

SOUND: Toilet flushing.

ORLANDO runs in laughing, VENOM is trying to catch him.

VENOM: Orly, man! Orly! Fuck's sake…

ORLANDO: Can't catch me! Can't catch me! I'm slippy as a eel!

EGGY: What the fuck are you doing, cuz?

VENOM: Trying to get him to wash his hands, man! Orly!

EGGY: Orlyyyy!

EGGY holds out a lollipop – ORLANDO heads straight for it…

ORLANDO: Mmmmmmm…!

EGGY: (*Snatching it out of reach.*) Dirty hands don't hold lollipops!

ORLANDO runs to the bathroom…

What in hell are we doing?

VENOM: Fuck knows man.

SOUND: Tap running...

VENOM: What if he pisses himself, man?

EGGY: You'll handle it, cuz.

VENOM: Me? You're the one what's got kids!

EGGY: Yeah, but he ain't my kid! I don't hardly touch them – I ain't gonna be wiping sweetboy's arse am I?

VENOM: You don't touch your kids, man?

EGGY: Your daddy touch you? No, me neither, and we turned out fine, innit? I love 'em an all dat but touching 'em just ain't neccessary. Fuck this man, why you sweating me? I thought we come out of prison, still.

VENOM: Takes more than a key, cuz. If you don't want to do this, why we here?

EGGY: So you don't go to Hell.

The Crossbar

KEVAN is waiting in a cute outfit holding two beers. JJ arrives – stands in the doorway, watching as KEVAN finishes a beer. JJ turns and leaves. KEVAN turns to the door – no JJ. KEVAN starts on the second beer.

Outside the Click Club

DANIEL giving out flyers.

DANIEL: Music not murder! Ragga not Rage!

SAM hurries up.

SAM: I'm here, I'm here – Music not murder! Beats not beatings! Sorry – Poor Daniel – you shouldn't have been left to take on the enemy alone.

DANIEL: Actually, everyone's been cool.

SAM: Well, what about those?

He points to red stains on DANIEL's shirt.

DANIEL: Oh, those? Just tomatoes. There's been a couple of drive-bys…

SAM: They were jealous of your cute outfit.

DANIEL: Of all the words in the English language you could select to describe me, I don't think anyone would choose cute.

SAM: Then let's see if we can come up with a new word specially for you.

DANIEL: Oh dear. I'm just going to fuck it all up again, aren't I?

SAM: We'll see.

KEVAN storms up and snatches a bunch of flyers.

KEVAN: Music not murder! Rhymes not crimes!

SAM / DANIEL: (*Exchanging a look.*) Hi.

KEVAN: Hi – Music not murder! Tracks not attacks!

SAM: Are you okay?

KEVAN: Oh, I'm great. Just wicked. No fucking boyfriend, no fucking life, but hey, no brain damage! 'Okay'? I'm downright lucky! Music not murder! Verses not hearses!

KEVAN, DANIEL & SAM move on as VENOM and EGGY enter in a hurry, VENOM holding ice lollies…

EGGY: What the fuck have you done with him?

VENOM: I only turned away for one second to pay the ice-cream geezer – Orly was right behind me being Tinker Bell sprinkling magic dust.

EGGY: 'Tinker Bell'?

VENOM: You know – Tinker Bell! Peter Pan's fairy friend!

EGGY: Fuck's sake!

VENOM: What we gonna do, man? He ain't never gonna believe it was an accident is he?

JJ: Accident?

EGGY: JJ bruv!

JJ: Accident? (*Looks round.*) Where's Orly?

EGGY: JJ bruv, it's cool…

JJ: Cool?! WHERE THE FUCK IS ORLY, YOU MURDERING BLACK BASTARDS? ORLY!

EGGY: JJ! Hear me, yeah?

JJ stares at EGGY wild-eyed.

Orly is fine. He is here – somewhere – and we will find him, bruv. We will find him.

EGGY, JJ & VENOM run off in separate directions

EGGY / JJ / VENOM: ORLY!

ORLANDO enters giggling, trying to find somewhere to hide.

ORLANDO: Ninety seven! Ninety eight! Ninety nine…

ORLANDO almost collides with a silhouetted figure – Light reveals a hooded WHITE FANG – he wears an eye-patch.

Julian?

WHITE FANG hurries away… ORLANDO goes after him…

Julian! Julian! You caught me! You caught me! Here I am! You won!

WHITE FANG: What the fuck are you talking about?

ORLANDO: The game! You found me and you won! You are so clever! Duran and Marky'll be so jealous!

WHITE FANG: Who?

ORLANDO: You know. Duran & Marky – Eggy and Venom.

WHITE FANG: Are they here?

ORLANDO: Somewhere. (*Whispers.*) I think they're lost. What's wrong?

WHITE FANG goes to leave, ORLANDO darts in his way again.

Aren't you friends no more?

WHITE FANG: Will you just fuck off out of my way, please?

ORLANDO: Why are you scared?

WHITE FANG: What the fuck do you want from me?

ORLANDO: I want to be friends.

WHITE FANG: Friends? You really have got brain damage.

ORLANDO: I want to know what happened to your eye. It wasn't Duran or Marky was it? I'm sure they never meant it. Did they hurt you, Julian?

VENOM comes running in.

VENOM: Orly, my brother! Where the fuck?

They exchange an elaborate handshake.

ORLANDO: Whassup bredren!

VENOM sees WHITE FANG.

VENOM: Fang?

ORLANDO: We've been playing, Marky – Julian won. Marky Mark, did you hurt Julian?

VENOM: What?

ORLANDO: You heard – If you did anything to hurt him, even by accident – you should say sorry. And you two should kiss and make up.

WHITE FANG: It wasn't him. I did it all myself.

ORLANDO: You cut out your own eye? Why?

WHITE FANG: It offended me. I was hanged up with a bunch of white blokes who didn't like niggers.

ORLANDO: But we're all niggas.

WHITE FANG: Speak for yourself. I was just an honorary nigga – A nigga once removed. When I found myself needing to stab me a fellow Negro in order to appease the Caucasian hordes – I couldn't do it. I'd rather cut out my eye than deface his precious blackness. Blackness was next to Godliness and I was just a pale-faced little Jewboy. Joke is – it's not as if I even liked niggers really. Yeah, I wanted to be seen with 'em – like

a chav wants to be seen with a pitbull on a chain – yeah,
I thought I wanted to be one – they made victimhood
so much funkier than us. We were all angst, they were
about attitude – We kvetched, they rapped. They
were cool. My grandparents met in a concentration
camp and yet five years after the war they had their
own shipping firm in Wapping. Black people are still
recovering from slavery three hundred years ago – but
to me they were cool – when the truth is that being a
nigger is just so three hundred years ago. My liberal
parents would die if they heard me talk like this – if
they hadn't already disowned me. My dad's flash law
firm takes legal aid cases and my mum does social work
at a women's prison – They listen to Aretha and Otis
– they love Mandela, Malcolm X, Martin Luther King
and Oprah – oh, they love the schwartzes – but the
blacks don't love 'em back. 'Cause they know the truth
– don't you, MC Venom? You know that white liberals
are just racists without balls. We can worship you, we
can demonize you – but we can never stand beside
you without adoration, envy, contempt or fear. Innit?
Blood?… Peace.

WHITE FANG leaves.

ORLANDO: Peace out, my nigga!

VENOM: Let's just get you home, little man, yeah?

EGGY comes striding up.

EGGY: Fuck's sake!

*EGGY & VENOM head straight for ORLANDO and scoops
him up between them…*

ORLANDO: Bredren!

*ORLANDO initiates the elaborate handshake, EGGY
declines…*

EGGY: Yeah, yeah, fairy boy, let's go!

EGGY grabs ORLANDO by the hand, realises himself and lets go.

KEVAN: Oy!

KEVAN heads over to EGGY, VENOM & ORLANDO.

What the fuck do you think you're doing?

EGGY: Wondering who the fuck you are.

KEVAN: Who the fuck am I? Who the fuck are you?

DANIEL and SAM head over to join them...

DANIEL: Kevan – Duran, Duran – Kevan...

KEVAN: I'm his friend, who the fuck are you? Come on Orly.

EGGY: Who the fuck am I? Just the nigga who's gonna hospitalize you, muthafucka.

DANIEL: Okay, Duran, there's no need for for this...

VENOM: He's right, Eggy man – ain't no need to escalate, alright?

KEVAN: 'Eggy'? Fucking 'Eggy'? Okay, you know what, take your fucking hands off him, alright?

DANIEL: Kevan.

EGGY: Or what?

KEVAN: Or I'm gonna have to be the muthafucka who hospitalizes you, nigger.

EGGY & VENOM share a look of disbelief.

EGGY / VENOM: 'Nigger'?

KEVAN: Nigger! N – I – G – G... E-R!

DANIEL / SAM: ... Oh dear.

VENOM: Oh, you silly white bitch – Gwan!

VENOM swings jokily at KEVAN – who dodges...

DANIEL / SAM / EGGY: Whoa!

EGGY: Whooo, it's oooon!

KEVAN: Come on, come on, best shot!

SAM: (*Rescuing ORLANDO.*) I'll look after you, pet – no charge.

KEVAN: Best shot, best shot! You think white men can't jump? Think again, yeah? KnowhatImean? You get me?

DANIEL: Okay, time gentlemen... Kevan...

KEVAN: You fucking get me?

KEVAN punches. DANIEL goes down.

ALL (NOT ORLY): Shit!

KKK's flat

KARISMA hurries into the romantically lit room – she holds two glasses of wine and wears a man's suit.

KARISMA: Sweetheart!

SOUND: Car horn.

KKK: (*Offstage.*) I know! One minute!

KARISMA opens the door, calls out...

KARISMA: One minute mate! Babycakes!

How long you gonna be in that bathroom?

Taxi's outside!

KKK: I know!

KARISMA: ... Bleedin' women...

KKK: Possess your soul with patience, man...

KKK enters in a dress and full make up.

... Beauty takes time, you know what I mean?

KARISMA stares.

KARISMA: Oh my God... Dijon... All is forgiven.

KKK: Dionne. Tonight I'm Dionne.

KARISMA: You're beautiful.

She goes to kiss him... KKK turns his head.

KKK: Mind the lips!

KARISMA takes his hand and kisses it... they entwine arms and drink.

SOUND: Door unlocking.

EGGY (*Offstage.*) Raaatid, man! Don't drop the muthafucka!

KKK and KARISMA stare at one other wide-eyed.

KARISMA: Bathroom!

KKK nips into the bathroom just as EGGY, VENOM, SAM & KEVAN burst in, carrying an unconscious DANIEL, ORLANDO sprinkling them with fairy dust the whole time.

EGGY: Crazy white faggot weighs a ton, man!

SAM: Why aren't we at the hospital?

VENOM: These is nearer, innit?

EGGY: You know how long an ambulance takes to reach New Cross?

VENOM: Fucking hell, little man, is wha' you have to hit him so hard for?

KEVAN: You started it!

EGGY: You got anger-management issues, man!

DANIEL: Uhhhh!

SAM leans over DANIEL.

SAM: Daniel?

DANIEL lifts his head and kisses SAM deeply. EGGY and VENOM look away.

EGGY: … Fuck's sake, man!

After a few moments, EGGY peeks, looks away…

Fuck's sake!

With a gasp, DANIEL loses consciousness again, head hitting the ground with a bang. SAM pulls himself together.

SAM: Water.

VENOM: Bathroom.

VENOM starts toward the bathroom, KARISMA blocks the way.

KARISMA: Bathroom's occupied!

EGGY: And who the fuck are you?

KARISMA: Dionne's Girlfriend.

EGGY / VENOM: 'Dionne'?

KARISMA: Dijon! I'm Dijon's girlfriend.

VENOM: He only come out of prison this week!

DANIEL coughs.

SAM: Water!

DANIEL: I'm fine!

DANIEL pulls SAM into another kiss, EGGY recoils...

EGGY: Fuck's sake! Water!

KARISMA: Kitchen! It's only upstairs!

VENOM: Fuck that! Dijon! Open the door, blood! It's me!

KARISMA: Dijon's sick! I'll go up and get it..

VENOM: Dijon, man!

KKK opens the bathroom door and comes out.

Dijon?

KEVAN: Dijon Socrates Lawrence the third? AKA Krazy Kop Killer?

VENOM: Lord Jesus Christ, Babylon reach!

KKK: Hey, you lot, Whassup?

EGGY: 'Whassup'? 'Whassup'? You stan' there looking like a down-low J-ho and you have the nerve to arx us 'whassup'? What the fuck is goin' on?

KARISMA: None of your business. You don't have to explain yourself, Dijon.

EGGY: And who the fuck is this irritating bitch? Your boyfriend?

ORLANDO: His lover.

All look at ORLANDO – who has suddenly grown up again.

Am I right? That's your lover? (*Approaching KARISMA.*) I'm Orlando. Pleased to meet you.

SAM: Shit! JJ!

SAM, EGGY, KEVAN & VENOM whip out mobiles and speed-dial.

KARISMA: Pleased to meet you. I've heard so much about you.

KEVAN: JJ mate! Where are you?

KEVAN ducks out of the room.

KARISMA: I'm Karisma.

ORLANDO: And this is Dionne?

KKK: Well, I couldn't decide between Dionne and Diane.

ORLANDO: Why not both? Dionne Diane Socrates Lawrence… The first.

KKK: You do know who I am, yeah? You know what I've done?

ORLANDO: Do you believe that's who you are? What you've done?

KKK: What else can I be?

KEVAN re-enters…

KEVAN: He's down the road at the Click Club – he's on his way.

KKK: I'm sorry. For what I've done. And ashamed. I'm ashamed. So sorry, so ashamed...

ORLANDO: Why be ashamed, when you can do something else? And become that?

KKK: Maybe that's what I'm trying to do.

EGGY: So what, you're gay now?

KKK: No blood, I ain't gay.

KARISMA: Trust me, he ain't gay.

EGGY: Trust you? You turned him into a woman!

KKK: I ain't trying to be a woman, bredren.

EGGY: You can't call me bredren dressed like that, man!

SOUND: Car horn.

KARISMA: I better pay that taxi off.

She exits...

EGGY: You were going out like that?

KKK: We were going to a ball.

EGGY: A ball? Okay, Cinderfella, I admit it – I do not get it. Help me understand, yeah? What the fuck?

KKK: Ain't you got a feminine side?

EGGY: If I have, it don't look like that, alright?

VENOM: What does it look like?

KEVAN: A lady truckdriver, probably.

EGGY: Fuck off! That's his job! I dunno, do I?

ORLANDO: Actually, you do.

EGGY: I do?

ORLANDO: You do. It looks like love.

EGGY: Like what?

VENOM: He says it looks like love, cuz.

EGGY: You lot just come away from me, yeah? Alla you just too damn sissy!

VENOM: So what if it looks like a lady truck driver? A lady's a lady, innit?

EGGY (*To VENOM.*) You stay out of it, you get me? You alright, dread? Ain't concussed or nuttin'?

DANIEL: I'm fine, thanks.

KEVAN: I'm sorry I hit you, mate…

DANIEL: So am I. Sort of…

DANIEL kisses SAM.

EGGY: Fuck's sake!

KARISMA enters with JJ.

JJ: Orly?

ORLANDO: JJ?

EGGY: Oh God.

JJ grabs ORLANDO in his arms…

ORLANDO: Where've you been, Rudeboy?

JJ: Looking for you, Orly.

ORLANDO: I'm just here.

JJ: Yes. You are. Oh God, Orly… There's so much I want to ask and now it's all flown away. Orly. I miss you Orly. I love you.

ORLANDO: There's something wrong with me, isn't there?

JJ: There's nothing wrong with you.

ORLANDO: Yes there is. I'm sorry.

JJ: There's nothing wrong with you Orly. You're perfect.

They kiss.

EGGY: Oh man!

EGGY turns away to find KARISMA & KKK kissing…

Oh man!

DANIEL & SAM kiss.

Fuck's sake! (*Eyes meeting VENOM's.*) What the fuck you looking at?

ORLANDO laughs and breaks away from JJ.

ORLANDO: Urrrr! JJ! He put his tongue in my mouth!

JJ: Orly?

ORLANDO: JJ kisses bo-oys! JJ kisses bo-oys!

JJ: No, Orly… only you.

ORLANDO: (*Whispers.*) It's alright… We won't tell! (*to the others.*) Will we?

JJ: It's okay, I don't mind…

ORLANDO wanders round the room, looking up at the walls…

ORLANDO: JJ kisses bo-oys… Man, look at all these records! Hundreds and hundreds and thousands and millions! Whose are they?

KKK: They're mine.

ORLANDO: Yours? Wow! You must be a millionaire! Can I play one?

KKK: Sure.

ORLANDO tries to scrunch a record onto the turntable.

VENOM: Let me, yeah?

He puts on the record, scratches it flashily and spins it.

SOUND: Music – 'Lion man'.

ORLANDO: Ohhh! Lion Man! (*Dancing.*) Let's dance! Everyone has to dance! (*Looks round.*) What's wrong?

JJ steps forward and stops the record.

JJ: It's Lion Man, Orly. He doesn't like us.

ORLANDO: Well, then we just have to love him more, innit?

JJ: It's too disappointing, Orly. You get into the rhythm, you're dancing happy for that first minute and then the lyrics kick you in the teeth.

ORLANDO: Well, before the lyrics there's the music, JJ. And the music is innocent, isn't it?

JJ: Maybe…yeah.

ORLANDO: Then if we just dance to the music, so are we. Let's dance, JJ – Just for a minute, yeah? Is wha'y'say, star?

JJ: I say…lyrics.

JJ re-starts the record, ORLANDO dances round him. JJ watches a moment, smiling, and then starts to dance with ORLANDO – swept up in by his lover's joy. VENOM is nodding his head, watching them. EGGY gives VENOM a warning punch in the arm. VENOM, ignores him, moving out of range, nodding some more. KARISMA holds a hand out to KKK – who takes it, allowing her to draw him into a winding, grinding slo-dance. VENOM is starting to move more now, getting into the rhythm... SAM crooks a finger, beckoning DANIEL to his feet. He takes DANIEL's hand and leads him into a step...and they dance. JJ reaches out to pull KEVAN in to dance with both him and ORLANDO. Reluctant at first, KEVAN can't resist being infected by ORLANDO's smile and he starts to dance. VENOM heads for his cousin, he grins at him, EGGY kisses his teeth, looks away, then looks round, shaking his head but before he can edit himself – he is smiling. VENOM laughs – pointing at him. EGGY gives in... He starts to move – and everyone is dancing.

Music break... and as the lyric kicks in...

Blackout.

End